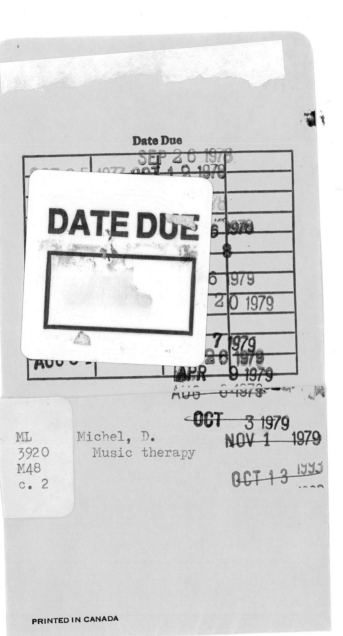

MUSIC THERAPY

MUSIC THERAPY

An Introduction to Therapy and Special Education Through Music

By

DONALD E. MICHEL, Ph.D., R.M.T.

Texas Woman's University
Denton, Texas
Formerly, The Florida State University
Tallahassee, Florida

CHARLES C THOMAS • **PUBLISHER**
Springfield • *Illinois* • *U.S.A.*

Published and Distributed Throughout the World by

CHARLES C THOMAS ● PUBLISHER

Bannerstone House

301-327 East Lawrence Avenue, Springfield, Illinois, U.S.A.

©*1976, by* CHARLES C THOMAS ● PUBLISHER

ISBN 0-398-03518-0

Library of Congress Catalog Card Number: 75-33976

With THOMAS BOOKS *careful attention is given to all details of
manufacturing and design. It is the Publisher's desire to present books that are
satisfactory as to their physical qualities and artistic possibilities and
appropriate for their particular use.* THOMAS BOOKS *will be true to those
laws of quality that assure a good name and good will.*

Printed in the United States of America

R-1

Library of Congress Cataloging in Publication Data

Michel, Donald E
  Music therapy.

  Bibliography: p.
  Includes index.
  1. Music therapy. [DNLM: 1. Music therapy.
WM450 M623m]
ML3920.M48   615'.837   75-33976
ISBN 0-398-03518-0

To the memory of my parents,
Ed and Edna Michel, and to
Mary Jeane, Trilly, and Matt,
my patient family

PREFACE

THE purpose of this book is to provide a basic introduction and orientation to the field of music therapy and music in special education. It is intended for the beginning music therapy student in college and for college students majoring in other therapy or special education areas. Music education students, in addition, should find it useful, not only because many of them will be. working with special education classes as part of their school assignments but also because they may be introduced to applications from the music therapy field which will be useful in working with problem children they may find in some of their regular classes and music groups — bands, choruses, and the like. Finally, the book may be of interest to students contemplating a career in music therapy, and to laymen or volunteers in music therapy who are seeking basic information about the field.

The reader will find many specific ideas about how music therapy works, but the coverage is not intended to be comprehensive. In the last decade, the field of music therapy has developed rapidly and it would require a larger coverage than this volume to be more intensive about the field.

Since its earliest days in the USA the field of music therapy has had to define itself — over and over again. The term is not self-evident, that is, it does not refer to a therapy concerned with treating MUSIC (as in speech therapy). It is not as apparent as occupational therapy, almost redundant in its implication of the value of being constructively occupied; nor is it as apparent as physical therapy, which implies a physical approach to physical problems; nor even as apparent as recreation therapy, again, almost a redundant term. In fact, the term music therapy often as not is misleading. It infers a specialized study (to some people) or a performance of music as a discipline in itself, as being the therapy rather than the use of music in its context of the broad field of human interest and activity ... for everyman. Perhaps it should have been called "music therapy" to connote the more universal aspect of music, using a small "m" instead of the capital "M"? Worse still, the implication sometimes is that the field is a highly specialized one, applicable only to a few musically trained persons, or involved in the MUSIC education or training of people (in a formal way) for therapeutic purposes. With all these misunderstandings it is a bit surprising to find that the field has developed into the respected one it is today! Perhaps the constant explaining of what it is by music therapists has kept it from becoming too dull and commonplace? On the other side of the coin a possible advantage to the acceptance of the field has been the almost universal potential of people to accept the possible therapeutic value of music in their lives. The only disadvantage to this might be in the overreadiness of some persons to accept magical or mystical connotations of music, or to exploit such possibilities.

It seems important to present an introduction to music therapy as realistically as possible, that is, without lending credence to the connotation of it being a highly specialized field with respect to application, nor to one of its being a magical, mystical phenomenon. It is hoped instead that the reader will discover how broad the field is, and how widely it may be applied regardless of the musical background of any patient, client, or special student. Further, it is hoped that the reader may be able to discriminate between what is the ALMOST magical value of music as a therapeutic medium, and any mystical concept of music AS therapy.

Finally, it is desired that the reader will realize something of the wide scope of application of music therapy, not only because of the universality of music as human behavior, but also because of the versatility of the well-trained professional music therapist, who, as a person, may be quite as important in working in therapy or special education as his musical tools are, even to the point of where he might sometimes decide to use other approaches before he uses music in his work.

The organization of this book is along the conventional lines of human age categories. This is comparable to other books in the fields of education and health professions. The age categorization seems to serve well not only from the practical standpoint but also from the standpoint of many clinical and special education facilities which frequently are organized on the age/developmental basis.

Most of the material for this book has been drawn from the writer's experience in the field as a clinician (eight years in a psychiatric hospital setting), a teacher/clinician (inaugurating and developing bachelors and masters degree training programs for music therapists), and as a researcher. Not only personal experience, but the experience of students, colleagues — and most importantly, the experience of those receiving music therapy — has been incorporated and drawn upon. To all of these persons I owe a great debt of gratitude — not only for continuously teaching me about my field but also for keeping it perpetually alive and exciting for me. Perhaps as Masserman has said, I may be acting as their "amanuensis" in authoring this book, and that is my hope. Readers are urged to write to me their reactions and criticisms and thus become a part of this continuing amanuensis.

D.E.M.

CONTENTS

MUSIC THERAPY

CHAPTER 1

THE FIELD OF MUSIC THERAPY

INTRODUCTION

Upon hearing of an occupation or profession which is relatively unknown to him, like music therapy — and which is not easily pigeon-holed into one of the more common groups of occupations such as law, medicine, teaching, or plumbing — a person is likely to say, "music therapy — what's that?" And he or she wants an immediate, simple answer. Of course, if the professional music therapist could just say, "Oh, it's like being a music teacher," the questioner might be temporarily satisfied, but if he is a trifle more curious, or concerned, or perhaps career-seeking, he will want a more complete answer. For that type of answer, and for that type of person some of the following may help clarify that a music therapist is something *more* than a music teacher — even though teaching music may be part of what he does.

Since any profession must ultimately be defined in terms of those who train in it and follow it as a career, (there are no career entities, or just bodies of knowledge without *persons* involved in it), we shall examine music therapy from the standpoint of what and who a music therapist is, and what he/she does.

A music therapist is first a behavioral scientist. In a large sense a teacher also is, or *should* be a behavioral scientist. However, the teacher, unless in a "research" position, is seldom a "scientist" in dealing with the behaviors of his students, as desirable as this might be. If the music therapist is a behavioral scientist, music therapy is therefore definable as one of the behavioral sciences. It is not then, a pursuit of the Art of Music *for itself*. It is not *performance* of music as "an end in itself." (This usually means, to the scientist, for the approval of peers and audiences.) It is *not* teaching music, as such. A behavioral science *is* concerned with human behavior, in all its aspects, and what affects changes in that behavior or behaviors. It is based on a scientific approach, which means that it recognizes not only the possibility but the probability of change in its own basic concepts, based upon research. It seeks to find new concepts from scientific research methods of testing and measuring. In fact, the scientific method basically means questioning the old (but *not* necessarily discarding it just because of age) and seeking the new in a constantly unfolding of knowledge. The scientific method is objective, that is, it is concerned with extending observations and measuring phenomena observed. It attempts to avoid reliance on personal, "subjective" impressions. In therapy, the behavioral scientist not only attempts to apply the results of his research to change behavior but also is constantly interested and involved in evaluating and measuring his results. Research is a part of his way of life.

Psychologists, sociologists, anthropologists, and some biologists are also behavioral scientists. Others who *may* be called behavior scientists, or who rely upon the behavior sciences are speech therapists, audiologists, and special education teachers, such as those working with retarded or with physically handicapped children.

The distinction between Art and Science is not always clear. It is well recognized by professionals in the behavior sciences that the development of research designs, and the carrying out of scientific research, or even the treatment of patients, is an "art" in the usually accepted creative connotation of that term, that is, it is done skillfully, and arouses the approval and admiration of fellow scientists who can "appreciate" it. But art and science do differ greatly in their methods of investigation. Art generally depends upon subjective, introspective means for discovering truths while Science tries to become as non-subjective, as *objective,* as possible.

Music therapy allies itself with and depends upon the findings of other behavior sciences, as well as its own scientific research. It is concerned about man and his behavior, especially his behavior with music. The music therapist must not only know a lot about the behavior sciences in general, but also about the interactions of music and man. Finally, as a therapist, he must learn how to apply his special knowledge and skills to the problems of seeking to change behavior.

The field of music therapy is relatively young. As an organized specialty it has come into widespread use in the USA only since about 1946. Yet it has had a place in the beliefs of man from ancient times, and even in the so-called "primitive" tribes still existing today. Ask most people if they *think* music might have therapeutic powers and they are likely to say, "Oh yes, I can see how music affects people ... I know how it calms me when I'm all tensed up." Or, they might recognize that music also excites them ... as at dances or sports events. They might recall how music provides a kind of solace for the war-weary soldier in far off lands, when in moments of respite from battles he sings with his buddies, or listens to a mate play on his guitar or harmonica. They might mention how music affects groups of kids at summer camp, as they all sit around the campfire and sing.

Are these ordinary functions of music for us in our daily lives what music therapy is all about? In a way, yes, insofar as music affects behavior of man in general ways. But is it therapy? No more so than man's use of other ordinary stimuli such as fresh air and sunshine, in his daily living. Healthful, perhaps, but seldom therapy. By definition, therapy is different than merely the pursuit of pleasurable, helthful stimuli.

Therapy Defined

Dictionary definitions of therapy and related words give basic ideas of the specific meaning of the word, e.g., "therapeutic" means "to attend" and " ... of or relating to the treatment of disease or disorders by remedial agents or methods." Therapy is defined as " ... remedial treatment of bodily disorder ... (or) ... psychotherapy (as) an agency designed to bring about social adjustment" (Webster, 1963). Masserman finds in the Greek root of the word, therapy, the meaning "service," and states that " ... serving the best interests of a fellow human being, whether stranger, friend, client, or patient, is the purpose of all treatment as well as the hallmark of civilization" (1966).

Under the broadest definition, almost anything done for people who are in need of it may be called therapy, perhaps even the "garden therapy" of garden clubs, which is supplying flowers for hospital patients. However, when used by professionals, the term therapy usually has a more definite connotation, that is, there is a specific measure taken to alleviate pain and initiate improvement in specific health problems. It is in this sense that music therapy should be considered, i.e., its use to accomplish specific treatment goals.

An implied meaning of therapy is *change* — the bringing about of changes from undesirable, unhealthful, uncomfortable conditions to more pleasant ones. (A change from pain to less pain might be one way of putting it, although over-simplified.) In this sense, therapy has a similar definition to that of learning: "changed behavior." Modern concepts of therapy very closely relate, and sometimes *equate* therapy and learning.

Masserman states that therapy in the psychological sense is "... the science, techniques, and art of exerting a favorable influence on behavior disorders by every ethical means available" (p. 114), and defines psychotherapy as " ... the science and art of influencing behavior so as to make it (a) more compatible with social norms and (b) more efficient and satisfactory to the individual" (1966, p. 110). One can even extend these definitions to apply to physiological disorders, i.e., when the patient's basic problem seems weighted in that direction, in which case the use of drugs, surgery, and other such authorized, ethical means are appropriate. Remember, man is not ever simply *either* mentally or physically sick, but whatever the cause, he may "hurt all over."

A final assumption about therapy is that it is ultimately *individualized*. Granting that hospitalization itself, with the advantages of modern technology and services, is in its way therapy, individualization of procedures to meet the unique needs of the unique individual is generally presumed in our society today. Music therapy strictly defined then, is an *individualized procedure*, whether the technique is one-to-one, or group. Looking at the term music therapy as we have defined it in therapy terms — what about "music" — does that need definition?

Music Defined

Music may not need defining for some people. It just IS. "Everyone knows what music is!" they might say. But on second thought, does everyone? Do we all agree on whether "Rock" is music? Or, that electronic experimentation with sounds is music? Maybe what is needed is an objective definition of music, if that is possible. Consistent with our therapy definition we might begin with describing music as human behavior. As such, music can be thought of as various behaviors such as blowing, striking, or picking on some sound-producing thing which together are called music, or musical behavior.

It is produced by man with sounds from various sources, including himself, and it is put into a system which man labels "Music." It differs from other forms of organized sound, such as speech, in its special systems of organization. It is often used as a special kind of communication, which sometimes includes words, but which is usually more important at its non-verbal level. This level expresses feelings symbolically and depends upon the time and place in which particular men are living (cultural boundaries). Looking at the organized pattern of sounds called music in an objective way, one might note that it differs from other types of organized sounds, such as speech, in most cultures, in that it uses a greater variety of sounds, with a wider variety of loudness levels and rhythmic accents. Now, of course, there also is monotony in music as well as in speech — but this greater variety is apparent when looking at the overall scope of music in most societies.

Some say that music goes beyond other forms of communication, that if speech were sufficient for man, music would never have been invented. But about all that can be said in summary in a definition of music is that man, in all societies — past and present — seems always to have had some system of organized sound communication which he labels music, and which he recognizes as different from other systems of sound communication. One more thing — music is a social phenomenon which depends upon the agreement of more than one person if the sounds are indeed "music." Exactly how many persons must agree is a moot point — depending upon societal boundaries. In a very permissive society people may grant to every individual his "right" to label anything he wishes as *his* music. Yet, if the sounds serve the basic purpose of communication with others, there must be some agreement — and as we all know, most of what is called music in our own society does gain agreement of many more than even two persons!

Perhaps music's unique influence which gives it such value in therapy lies in the fact that it is a form of human behavior, which is uniquely labelled, and which is used by man as a communicative medium, differently than other media. Generally, it is enjoyed as a pleasurable activity, and thereby it serves well as reward (or reinforcement) in therapeutic use. However, the other side of the coin is that music also can be painful sometimes, for some individuals. (Its negative use is suggested in this, but has rarely been experimentally tested.)

Music is nearly always structured within quite precise time boundaries and this makes it useful as a medium for structuring activities, especially learning activities. It can be structured in small bits of time as well as in extended time structures. Finally, music is a medium widely used by man for social communication and social intercourse — a unique use which makes it a valuable therapeutic medium.

RECENT HISTORICAL PERSPECTIVES

Music Therapy as an Activity Therapy

It is of some interest and significance to look at music therapy, now that we have defined it basically, as a field which has had its development as a profession mostly since the end of World War II (1946). This is particularly true in the Western world, especially the USA, where a group of therapies known as Activity or Adjunctive Therapy developed. Usually included in this grouping are occupational therapy (which has the oldest history), physical therapy (which in some form has existed for a longer time, also), recreational therapy, educational therapy, corrective therapy, manual arts therapy, and bibliotherapy (the latter three having been developed mostly in veterans' hospitals).

The use of activities in treatment procedures has only had wide acceptance since World War II. Forms of occupational therapy, music therapy, and recreational therapy in institutions have existed in isolated situations since before the 1940's, but were usually considered to be mostly a humane way for patients to while away long hours of "convalescence," rather than as specific media for therapy.

In the field of mental health in the mid-1940's, when music therapy began to be used as a specialty, *psychotherapy* was considered by most medical authorities to be the prerogative of the psychiatrist, almost exclusively. Any other ways of working with patients were considered to be at best "supportive." Even clinical psychology in the immediate post-World War II years was considered "supportive," and its chief role that of diagnostic testing. Social work was supportive in the sense of providing useful case history material to the psychiatrist and in dealing with troublesome family and relatives. Although in clinical work during that time some psychiatrists referred to psychotherapy facetiously as "talking" therapy, the belief generally held was that psychotherapy was really the only thing which helped patients.

More reliance gradually was placed upon activities, sometime called the "adjunctive" or "ancillary" therapies, to help patients. The team concept in therapy began to grow, with cooperation being sought between the various persons who had contact with the patient. This was not only related to the necessities and realities of institutional life, but also to a concept called *milieu therapy,* or the attempt to control the environmental contacts of the patient in order to influence behavior changes. *Milieu therapy* was highly developed and organized by the Menninger Foundation in Topeka, Kansas, even to the extent of setting up "attitude therapy" in which the milieu, especially the interpersonal contacts of the patient with the staff, was "controlled" (See *Guide to the Order Sheet,* 1950). This was done by carefully describing attitudes and other procedures which were consistently to be taken with individual patients *by all therapists* on the team. From this came the idea that activity therapies should be individually "prescribed" by the team "leader," usually the psychiatrist.

"Prescribed" activities therapy, in the sense of striving for some consistency in working with patients, is still being practiced in many places. The difference today, however, is that activity therapy often is the therapy of choice, not just supportive, ancillary, or adjunctive. The qualified activity therapist is an important contributing member of treatment teams, and frequently participates in decision-making concerning the patients, including diagnosis and the "prescription" of a therapy program (Michel, 1965).

Perhaps three things have influenced this change. One is the recognition and wider acceptance of learning theory as a part of psychotherapy. Insight might still be considered an important way of learning and for influencing behavior change, but reconsidered ideas of learning derived from behavior conditioning theories (Pavlov, Watson, Skinner, *et al.*) as accomplished through procedures which are easily adapted by therapists, gave new importance to activity therapy.

The second influence came from a recognition that at the heart of activity therapy is the interpersonal relationship — or rapport — between therapist and patient, which has always been considered an important facet of psychotherapy. The third influence probably relates to Stan Boucher's "RURPP" concept[1] which symbolizes the increasing recognition of needs for therapy in our population (1967). As Boucher said, the tranquilizer and energizer drugs, developed and used in mental health in the 1950's, served to make more patients amenable to psychotherapy, rather than accomplishing miraculous cures. Government-sponsored medical treatment for more people also is a big factor. Psychiatrists and other "traditional" therapists cannot meet all the demands being made upon their time. The only answer seems to be increased reliance upon other types of "helpers" — especially activity therapists. (This will be discussed further in Chapter IV.)

The Evolution of a Profession

In music therapy, as an attempt to describe the progress up to 1960, the field was alluded to as a person, or a patient who was

---

[1]Referring to "Realistic Ultimate-Reality Patient Population."

rapidly "getting well" (Michel, 1960). The National Association for Music Therapy (NAMT) was the "therapist" in this allegory, and the "case study" covered all the major "treatment" steps up to 1960. The conclusion was that music therapy had then begun to reach a mature, responsible level of professionalism.

Some writers have looked upon the "case-history" of music therapy as having ancient historical roots. They cite the Old Testament Bible, the Ancient Greeks, and the anthropologists who find and report treatment uses and beliefs about music as therapy in primitive and ancient societies. The details of these backgrounds will be omitted here, however, in favor of a summary of the present status of music therapy which may be seen through more recent development of professional standards. Most of these have come about through the NAMT.

The Registered Music Therapist (RMT) today must have completed four years of an academic program in an approved school, followed by a six months clinical internship in an approved music therapy program. The RMT classification is awarded by the NAMT and provides the basic standard for employment under civil service and merit systems in many states, counties, and cities. Graduate work is possible at the masters degree level and often emphasizes the development of research techniques (See *Music Therapy as a Career*, NAMT, 1975).

The music therapist today is a professionally trained person who knows how to use his unique medium, music, to influence desirable changes in his patients. He does not necessarily specialize with any particular age group although he may wish to do so by later experience and/or post-graduate study. He is not necessarily restricted to working with any particular type patient with particular disorders like behavioral, or retardation, although this too might become his specialty. Instead, he is a kind of generalist with special tools, *musical*, which he can adapt to the diagnosed needs of various patients. He may be a team member who contributes to both diagnostic and treatment procedures of patients within a modern clinical facility, or he may be in private practice, receiving patients on referral from clinics, from other professionals, or by self-referral.

The unique tool of the music therapist may be likened to a two-

edged sword, with one edge being the basic power of music as a
sound stimulus which stimulates or quiets; and the other edge the
uses to which man has put music, such as the social dance, or the
symbolic song of patriotism, religion, or fraternity.

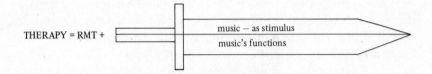

THERAPY = RMT +   music — as stimulus / music's functions

The skillful music therapist makes use of both edges of the sword,
shifting the emphasis from one side to the other or using both
simultaneously. In addition to becoming a skillful manipulator
of this musical sword, the modern RMT must be competent in
basic therapeutic knowledge and skills. He must learn how and
when his skills can be combined toward changing behavior in a
patient.

One further question may be asked about the music therapy
professional: When would a patient *need* a music therapist?
When would music therapy be most indicated? Is it possible to say
that there may be times when a patient needs music, or therapy
through music, more than anything else, or perhaps even exclusive of other things? Certainly the most common situation would
be in a clinical setting where assessment and agreement by the
team would indicate music therapy as one part of a multi-faceted
program, utilizing several media. Here it would be seen that music might add another dimension to speech therapy, for example,
or that it might provide the most subtle means, or most compatible with the patient's interests and background (*not* necessarily
his abilities), for carrying out treatment aims toward which the
focus of all treatment was directed.

But again, in its unique, especially its *extra-verbal* functions
for and with man, music might well be the means of choice. Its
very nature as a form of communication might make it first
choice, e.g., for the patient who has been overstimulated or un-
reached by more direct, obvious means, such as verbal language.

For the person who decides what the therapy should be for a

patient (psychiatrist, physician, psychologist, or the entire "team" including the music therapist), therapy through music could very well be the therapy of choice, and at times, perhaps, even exclusive of other approaches. More specific answers to the question of when a music therapist is needed are being provided through current research efforts. As treatment of various disorders becomes more focused *outside* of institutional settings the skills of music therapists become more needed. One example is the increasing demand for music therapists in special education programs in the public schools, where the RMT's may serve as resource and demonstration persons for special education classroom teachers as well as for music teachers assigned to work with these classes.

CHAPTER 2

MUSIC THERAPY FOR CHILDREN AND ADOLESCENTS

How does anyone come to need therapy? It might be helpful at this point to conceptualize what health and illness is all about. The following diagram is based upon Selye's concept of stress as the primary factor involved (Selye, 1956).

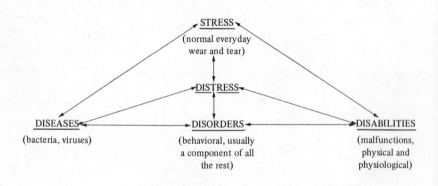

CONCEPT OF ILLNESS

The above chart applies equally well to all ages. It reminds us that a person suffering from any dislocation of equilibrium, of homeostasis, or of "good adaptation" (good health), normally encounters stress, which *may* ultimately become *distress*. Distress may also become or be a product of either a disease, disorder, or a disability. Disorder is shown in the middle because nearly all diseases and disabilities manifest themselves in some sort of behavioral disorder, and this is often a starting place, as well as a final stage in treatment. Sometimes disorders become the primary problem of the distressed individual. It may be said that

14

"behavioral" disorders are basically social disorders in that they are manifested in the relationships of the individual in interaction with others. The term "behavior disorder" is often used as a synonym for "mental illness" or "emotionally disturbed" and is now frequently the preferred label.

HEALTH PROBLEMS OF CHILDREN AND ADOLESCENTS

Health problems of children are often developmental in nature, i.e., they are related to the growth or developmental patterns of children. This applies to *diseases* in the sense that children seem to be most susceptible to certain viruses and other diseases at certain ages (3 - 12 years — pre-school and elementary school), such as formerly was true of measles and is still true of mumps, whooping cough, and chicken pox.

The same applies to *disorders*, that is, behavior disorders, which may develop as a part of the socializing process in children. For some, development is short circuited or distorted, and the child learns behaviors which are considered disturbed or disordered. These behaviors usually are distressful to himself or to others.

Disabilities likewise seem to occur with some typical patterns in children as part of the developmental process. From birth, some children are disabled by brain damage (e.g., cerebral palsy), others suffer intellectual disablement or impairment from some prenatal, birth, genetic, or unknown causes. Childhood accidents result in disabilities of various kinds, from crippled limbs to brain damage. Some disabilities stem from diseases, such as poliomylitis, and encephalitis and other severe viral diseases. Such diseases are more common in children than in adults.

There are some disturbances which result in disorders and/or disabilities in children which are either congenital or at present little understood as to origin. One such disorder is called *Early Infantile Autism* and seems to be more of a behavior disorder than a disease or a physical disability. Disturbed behavior is exhibited, such as: the child does not communicate with people, has many stereotyped, ritualistic behaviors, and has severe deficits in learning and socializing.

Adolescent problems are sometimes the result of continued childhood diseases, disorders, or disabilities originating at earlier ages, but the great physiological and glandular changes occurring in adolescence contribute special circumstances which bring on problems peculiar to this stage of growth. Very often, these problems are reflected in the area of social relations — the adolescent to his peers, to his parents and other adults, and to society as a whole.

CONCEPT OF MULTIPLE HANDICAPS

No one is ever handicapped or disabled in one way only. There are always social and emotional components. This is sometimes called the *Concept of Multiple Handicaps*, i.e., any handicapping event affects more than one part of a person's functioning.

The term "rehabilitation," (like its length) usually implies a longer, continuing process than "therapy," but the two words are often used interchangeably.[1] No one is seldom "just crippled" from say, a broken limb. The whole social pattern of the individual with a broken leg is changed. Everyone knows it takes the "will to recover" from any kind of disturbance — broken bones, surgery, or crippling disease, or even the common cold. For certain disturbances, it takes longer to recover; for certain persons recovery is more difficult. In nearly all cases, long or short term, music *can* play a part in the recovery — both in specific applications to basic problems and in influencing the "will to recover" that is, motivation or "morale."

Music therapy for children and adolescents, then begins with a concept of the *multiple handicap* principle. Rehabilitation and/or therapy goals may focus upon primary and/or associated handicaps — in the physical, social, and behavioral (emotional) realms of the person. The music therapist may use his musical tools as structure to reinforce and organize physical coordination, or as reward for rehabilitative work tasks, or as a means for social participation and interaction — often all at the same time, to meet

---

[1]And sometimes together, i.e., activity therapists in California are called rehabilitation therapists (1974).

the multiple treatment needs of the patient.

CONCEPTS OF DIAGNOSTIC LABELING

Children and adolescents, like adults, are distressed by many problems in their adaptations to life, but we tend to group, for statistical and other reasons, problems and people into categories. These categories may describe the general problem area of the person, such as retardation, visual disability, hearing disorder, speech and language disorder, emotional or behavioral disorder, physical disability (sometimes divided into subcategories like sensory-motor problems), or social deviation (or similar terms which encompass juvenile delinquency, drug abuse, etc.). It is important to remember however that such labels are NOT necessarily *disease* categories for diagnostic purposes, as in medical problems. The labels are really only for the convenience of other persons who need a quick identification or grouping of persons with similar problems. That such "other persons" may also be subject to being labeled themselves, illustrates the point that it is a mistake to allow a label to be substituted for recognition of the PERSON with problems. The person is a unique, human individual, at least in this author's value system. Also to be remembered is the fact that individuals are likely to be distressed by more than one handicapping condition i.e., they may be multiply-handicapped, which makes any one label of any kind greatly inadequate. Even the term multiply-handicapped may be insufficient! How do you label a three-year-old child who was severely neurologically impaired at birth, has poor eyesight, and who seems to measure well below other average levels of development for three-year-olds? Is he retarded? Physically handicapped? Visually disabled? Sensory-motor impaired? Or, all of these? Confronting this sort of dilemma, one may quickly see the absurdity of relying on any single label if one wishes to be able to help the individual child.

A child with all these problems may very well be found in a hospital or training center for "retardates," or he may be found as a client of an Easter Seal rehabilitation center for physically handicapped. He might be found in a community center for treatment of children with sensory-motor disabilities where he may be brought daily for treatment. His labels, his disorders and/or disabilities — nor even their severity — do not determine *where* he may receive treatment. And it may realistically be said that wherever he is found is probably not directly due to whatever label may be attached to him, but rather due to the social circumstances into which he is born, i.e., whether or not his family can cope with his problems, or how they may cope with them. In other words, retarded children are not found in institutions for the retarded because of their retardation. They are there because of circumstances of their birth, such as whether or not parents, or other family, can take care of them at home.

If one looks at the handicapped child as an individual who needs help, one must look further than the label under which he finds the child. This means we must identify objectively the problems of the individual which are reflections of the handicapping condition and at the same time may actually *be* the handicapping condition. For example, our three-year-old child may first need to learn to respond better to an adult helper: teacher, doctor, music therapist, or whoever, and this might be accomplished by working directly in a planned program to increase the amount of attention, or "attending behavior" of the child.

A typical session in such a program might proceed like this: "Look here, Johnny." . . . "Good boy!" (Therapist may reward Johnny's attention with candy, or with music, or with back-patting, or other things Johnny has indicated he likes.) If Johnny responds with increasing amounts of attention, and the professional therapist will make sure whether or not progress is being made by keeping careful records and measuring the changes, he may well be on his way toward developing his individual potential, since learning begins with attention. And if Johnny attends, more and more, for longer and longer periods, he is learning how to learn. A music therapist can be important in this process, using music to demand Johnny's attention in increasing amounts of time, or by rewarding Johnny with his favorite music such as listening, playing a jingle bell, or an autoharp, for paying attention.

Let us look at some of the problems, treatment, and treatment facilities found with children like Johnny. The concept of multiple handicaps has already been discussed and it was noted that a *primary* disability, disorder, or disease often is the determining factor with respect to the label which may be given to the child (or, to his problem). If the primary disability is the child's general inability to learn like other children do who are his chronological age, and he seems generally slow in developing physical coordination (motor skills) in comparison with his peers, he may be given the general label of retarded. However, remember that such a general label tells us very little about a child like Johnny. In order to help him we must know more specifically what his problems are. Nevertheless, the general label may help determine that Johnny is to be treated in an institution for the retarded. Remember also, that it probably is *not* even this label which determines whether or not Johnny will be institutionalized but rather the social circumstances in which he exists. His family may be unable or unwilling to cope with Johnny, so he is put into an institution. What are the problems he comes with and how are they dealt with?

PROBLEMS AND TREATMENT OF CHILDREN WHO ARE "RETARDED"

Whether or not a child like Johnny is institutionalized, his basic problems are pretty much the same as if he were being treated at home, in a community or regional center, or in special classes in school — at least in the beginning. At early chronological ages, early in the developmental phase, a child's problems may be those of basic adaption to the social expectations and demands of his immediate environment, e.g., toilet-training (bladder and bowel, voluntary control). However, these problems may also be found in handicapped children at other ages.

Problems of adaptation which are preliminary to a child's engaging in other learning activities as a part of a group are called social-adaptive skills or self-help and self-care behaviors, like being able to dress and undress oneself, or being able to feed oneself. These problems must be dealt with in an environment in which the child is to be treated, before other learning problems can be attacked. Even basic skills such as self-dressing can be broken down into smaller parts which can be learned by a child who is handicapped, even one who is multiply-handicapped, such as our hypothetical Johnny. Music therapy may play an important part in teaching Johnny basic "pre-learning" skills and behaviors such as auditory discrimination of different sounds and words or maintaining eye-contact, or cooperating with another child. But the individualized concept of therapy, already mentioned, is the key concept. If Johnny is a resident of an institution, his care might first have to meet the problems of adapting to the institution before he can be given individualized treatment which is ultimately necessary for his progress.

In traditional training institutions for the retarded, treatment programs begin with a general, group-oriented approach, to meet the needs of the institution, which more often than not, are due to having only a minimum staff which is sufficient only to provide a general kind of care. Music programs in such institutions have long been a part of generalized "care," and the resident children have been exposed to music in group activities, in entertainment situations, and as background. Quite possibly, such exposure has touched responsive chords in some individuals, and in a general way, provided therapy for them. Or, in some instances, where group activities in music are conducted with the same individuals over a continuing period of time, individual needs may surface and be given special attention by music leaders or therapists, and in such a way, become more specific therapy for the individual.

From the great impetus given to the field of Retardation by the interest and support of President Kennedy in the USA during the 1960's, many institutions for the retarded have developed more sophisticated therapy programs, which are directed more toward individualized goals. In such institutions, music therapists work with children in small groups or classes of children with similar problems. They are put into groups of two to five, and individual needs are more easily noted and met.

In the first type of institution music therapy may have been established on the basis of its claims of meeting general goals of residents, such as physical stimulation or alertness training; improving physical coordination; providing socializing experiences; providing healthy outlets for expression of feelings; and providing self gratification for those who participate. Also, the well-known effect of music, which has been touted by writers for centuries — the soothing effect, or calming, restful, or sedative effect — may be a part of the rationale for such programs.

In more modern settings, some of these effects may only be claimed *if* they are meeting individual needs as specifically noted, and as particularly planned for in the music therapy sessions, or classes. Ideally, each individual child will have his own "prescribed" goals listed, toward which all therapists work to help him make progress. Such goals may be in the area of social adaptiveness or personal self-help skills, or they may be specified in terms of basic social behaviors the child needs in order to function and learn in a small group. Goals may also be in the area of academic skills, like reading and writing.

An example of how music therapy helped one child is in the story of Timmy, and his learning to care for himself, so he could be ready to leave his ward and go to education classes, specifically, by being able to put on his own clothes. One "small" problem for Timmy was buttoning two buttons on his shirt-vest. The music therapist discovered that Timmy liked to play rhythm instruments while the therapist played the guitar. Timmy was then required to *try* to button his shirt *before* he was given rhythm instruments to play, as a reward. Carefully timed and planned amounts of effort were "paid-off" by appropriate timed amounts of music activity. Of course, Timmy did not succeed perfectly the very first time he tried, but as long as he kept trying, and made some approximations toward the end goal, he was given portions of music as a reward by the therapist. Ultimately, he succeeded!

In the *ideal* therapy setting, an individual child will have had precise diagnosis or pin-pointing of his specific problems and will have been given his own individualized program for improvement. Many experts believe that the ideal setting for most children with special problems is the home, that is, a home where there are informed parents or other relatives who have the time and ability to carry out such an individualized program. Since this is such a rare situation, variations from this ideal move outward toward the community, beginning with community-based clinics and centers. In such centers, the ideal situation would be one where parents could bring their child and could learn how to continue in the home the therapy provided by expert therapists in the clinic. This would also apply to special education facilities in schools.

The ideal situation is still seldom seen today. Too often the least ideal one is found where only minimum custodial care is provided for large groups of children. In such institutions, any effort away from the drabness of an everyday routine which maintains a sanitary existence for large groups of children, toward individual care can be considered progress toward the ideal. In any of these varied settings there is a role for the music therapist. Hopefully, it is one which strives toward the individualization of therapy for the children by the specification of their problems and the spelling out of special programs for each child.

When a handicapped child is a part of a special education program in the schools by virtue of his having been cared for at home, his having achieved a sufficient level of adaptation to enable him to participate in a school setting, or as a result of his having been selected from the school population for special help, for whatever reason, he may be involved in music experiences. What form should the music experiences take? WHO should provide them? Musicians? Music educators? Music therapists? What should be the role of music for handicapped children in the schools?

MUSIC IN SPECIAL EDUCATION: ENTERTAINMENT, EDUCATION, OR THERAPY?

From the preceding paragraphs, one may already presume that the answer to this question is not an absolute one, i.e., it is possible and desirable for handicapped children to participate in music in the same ways other children do. Music in some form is participated in by almost everyone to some degree. Like other parts of our lives, it is often taken for granted. Only if it is controlled or taken away do most people give it much thought, or consider its importance, its value to their lives. As recreation or entertainment it is enjoyed by millions in one form or another.

Like other forms of recreation it may become a serious, intensive pursuit for some, yet not be their full-time occupation or vocation. Like other forms of recreation, music may be the vocation, the fulltime occupation or profession for some people. Where does it fit in Special Education — special programs designed for handicapped children?

It may be convenient to consider music as a profession under three main headings: performing, education, and therapy. This is not foreign to other professions or occupations, which also may have their performance, education, and therapy components, e.g., speech and drama, or a whole range of occupations and crafts which are sometimes referred to as industrial arts, and become "occupational therapy."

Music therapy is defined as a behavioral science not only because music is human behavior but also because the use of music in therapy depends upon a mastery of behavioral skills in addition to those of performance and teaching, that is, upon the knowledge and skills necessary to relate the human activity of music to therapy goals. Music therapy today is a recognized profession which requires a specialized form of training. Like other professions, some of its techniques can be learned by nonprofessionals from other fields. Music therapists themselves learn techniques developed in other fields such as psychology, speech pathology, and special education. This does not make them professionals in these fields. Likewise, professionals in these fields can learn certain music therapy techniques without becoming professional music therapists. The health profession in general today needs many specialties and it also needs the sharing of special techniques among the various professional therapists who work together, ideally, as a "team." Nevertheless, roles need to be defined.

Perhaps this definition of role is the fundamental problem to be considered as music becomes increasingly available to the children who are taught in special education. It is a problem only because the therapeutic values of music have become more and more recognized and used in special education. Handicapped children have always had some kind of music, and often, it has been observed that many of these children respond in a special way to music.

As more attention to children with special needs has been given in the schools it was inevitable that music educators became involved in providing the music to which so many children, handicapped or not, respond. Music educators more and more are being asked to provide music experiences for the children who are in special education. But many music educators are finding that they, like the general classroom teacher, are not prepared to provide the special approaches for or respond to the special problems of these children.

There is a parallel in the recent history of the development of the field of music therapy itself. Patients in treatment institutions — like people outside institutions — were observed to be responsive to music which sometimes seemed to be "therapeutic." This became more noticeable by the general public as treatment of those persons with behavior disturbances ("mental illness") became better known as a consequence of the post-World War II treatment of returned veteran servicemen from the armed forces, (particularly in the victorious countries like the USA). The first provision of music for institutionalized patients was by persons who were professional musicians (performers), music educators, or amateur (but trained) musicians. These persons with music skills, but untrained in therapy procedures, were the founders of the field of music therapy. (Speech teachers and drama coaches likewise were the earliest speech therapists and drama therapists.) As training standards in music therapy became established, the music persons working in institutions and hospitals gradually became, or were replaced by music therapists.

Music provided for special children in schools up to now has largely been furnished by musician-performers and educators. More and more, music therapists are being employed in such work. The therapeutic values of music thus may become realized when applied by the trained music therapist. During the transition period in institutions and hospitals while music therapists were gradually replacing performing musicians and/or teachers, many of these persons took advantage of in-service training, part-time educational opportunities outside working hours, and other opportunities afforded by their work to become competent therapists. Will there be such a transition period with music in special education?

In actuality there already has been (and is continuing to be), such a transition period. Music educators working with special children in the schools have sometimes taken advantage of workshops, in-service training, and other opportunities to become more competent in providing music in a meaningful way with special children. In a few instances, music educators now are working under the guidance and direction of qualified music therapists and have been able to make the music experiences of their special children even more meaningful in terms of the needs of these children. Just as special education teachers sometimes provide resources, guidance, and direction to general classroom teachers who have some special children in their classrooms, music-therapists might be expected to increase such roles with music educators, as well as with classroom teachers, both special and general, in the near future.

In a transition period, there is sometimes a blurring of roles and goals, as the current practitioners continue to gain experience and newly-trained "experts" join their ranks. Experienced educators may see little difference in the new expert's approaches and their old ones; they may feel that in fact, "experience is the best teacher." This was the subject of many of the early participants in national meetings of music therapists in the 1950's. Some experienced music educators, who were working in institutions, expressed the view that music therapists needed only a little more training, PLUS experience, beyond the training they would receive in a music education college curriculum. Others, performing musicians who were working in institutions, believed that just a little more training PLUS institutional experience would be the best training for music therapists. (It is interesting to note as an aside that these two somewhat opposing viewpoints became the bases for theoretical discussions about where and how the "therapy" existed in music. The educators generally felt there was therapeutic value in the learning of music and in participating in large, learning groups, such as the bands and choruses found in schools, while the performing musicians generally felt that the value of music for and in therapy lay in the music itself, and in its performance. Music therapy viewpoints today do not wholly endorse either viewpoint.)

In music in special education, experienced music educators may feel that a somewhat modified training and role of music teacher can provide the special child with all the benefits presumed to be in the learning and experiencing of music. This is seen by them to be little different from music therapy procedures. Some may even believe music education procedures are better as or in therapy.

As music therapy gradually became differentiated from a special kind of music education or music performance for patients in psychiatric institutions, a recognition of the need for a different kind of training also occurred. Perhaps the change in music therapy education (for therapists) itself played a part in this differentiation process. Based on observed needs of the patients which dictated the music approaches and uses made by music therapists in hospitals and other institutions, this education or rather, the educational standards for music therapy training, evolved and continue to evolve as an entity quite different from the training curricula for educating music educators and music performers.

The fundamental question is: How do performance, education, and therapy differ? The answer may seem deceptively easy. Performance is performance. Education is education. Therapy is therapy. But all may be intertwined with each other. The value of a human activity which is performed by many and specialized in by a few is what is recognized by a society as important and that which is incorporated into its education system. That same value, plus others which may be similar, is sometimes what transforms an activity into a medium for therapy, and also, sometimes is that which involves the use of such a medium through education or teaching channels. Such seems to be the case in several areas of human activity which have evolved into activity therapy, e.g., physical exercise which is valued by many, specialized in by a few, taught as physical education in the schools, and becomes physical or exercise therapy when applied to the therapy needs of people. And so it is with music therapy. Performance and education procedures and techniques might well be employed, but the fundamental difference lies in NEEDS and GOALS of the patient.

These needs and goals are the *first* consideration in therapy, and very often determine a quite different approach than is customarily made if the activity is simply performance or is being taught (often toward performance goals). Music therapy makes use of performance, and of music education techniques, but requires a fundamentally different approach, as well as a very different background of knowledge than is necessary for performance or education. This is the basic answer to the question of what music in special education should be. It should not be entertainment (or performance) alone; it should not be music education alone; with today's level of development in the field, it *should be music therapy*.

In the foregoing paragraphs, an attempt has been made to provide a rationale for the use of music therapy in special education, rather than music entertainment or music education. The situation can be further clarified by citing some examples of how music therapy may work in a special education setting. It should be noted that there are many kinds of "special education settings." In schools in many places there is a tendency to try to provide for children on an individual basis, with special help furnished the exceptional or handicapped ones in accordance with their special needs in specific areas of their lives. The special education resource center within the school is one way of providing for such individual, specific needs, where a child may be referred for parts of his school day for special help in subjects such as reading, counting, writing, or basic skills involved with these competencies. During other parts of his day, the child may be with classmates of his own chronological age group, where his competencies are similar to those of his peers.

More familiar to most people is the special education classroom where the child spends his entire school day. In this kind of special education setting as well as in others such as the resource room, children most commonly have received music experiences from music educators. Another form of special education setting is found in special schools in the community, where all of the students are handicapped. Here music may also be provided by music educators, but music therapists are beginning to be a part of the special education staff in such schools.

Still another form of special education setting now is found in hospitals and training centers for handicapped children. The whole institution may be considered a form of special education, but there are special programs and classes, both in and out of classrooms in such institutions as those called "Sunland" in Florida. Here it is common to find music therapists regularly employed.

Examples

In each of these special education settings, music in therapy may have a prominent part in the habilitation and rehabilitation of special children. An example of one way it might be used is as a means of developing self-esteem in children whose problems are complicated by a definite lack of self-confidence. Self-esteem and self-confidence can be objectively measured and diagnosed through the use of certain paper-pencil tests and teacher observations, and, with such base line data as a starting point, music might be used with the objective of increasing self-esteem. A basic skill on an instrument, such as the ukulele or guitar, might be taught to a group of children, or to individuals, and after basic skills have been learned, such as being able to play chord accompaniments to familiar songs which the children can sing, measurement of self-esteem can be made again. If self-esteem has increased, the therapist would then develop procedures to make certain that the increased self-confidence was transferred and applied to other learning tasks, such as reading. In research studies, this approach has proven to be a promising use of music therapy in special education (Michel, 1970, 1971, 1973).

Would only a music therapist be able to carry out such procedures? As far as setting up the procedures, from obtaining base line data to measuring progress and choosing appropriate musical "tools," the music therapist is much better trained to do so. However, music educators and/or classroom teachers (special educators) might well be able to carry out some of the procedures which are repetitive on a day-to-day basis. Thus, the music therapist's specialized role might be further extended by allowing him additional time to be able to work in other special programs. The music therapist then would be functioning as a special resource person or consultant, much like other specialists such as speech pathologists, remedial reading teachers, or physical therapists. The music therapist thus would be able to serve many types of children in different kinds of special education settings as, e.g., classroom, resource center, special school, or special class in hospital or training centers.

Another example of how a music therapist might work in a special education setting is in helping special children accomplish basic learning skills or basic concepts. Here a music therapist might be asked to set up a particular learning procedure involving music, such as one developed in recent research, where music was used to help develop associations and labelling (naming), between paired objects from the child's environment. This is a form of the paired-associate learning technique, where familiar objects are paired with unfamiliar ones in a drawing or picture, and the familiar one used to help the individual learn and recall the name of the new object. Specially-composed melodic phrases using the names of the two paired objects learned by the individual can be a help in learning and remembering (Wilson, 1971). This sort of activity most likely would be developed and set up by a music therapist, but again, part of it might be carried out in daily practice by others such as a classroom teacher or a music teacher.

Another example which might be found in the setting of special education is one where severely emotionally disturbed children are given special help. Where attention to stimuli and auditory memory "sequencing" are found to be deficient in certain individual children (as diagnosed by special psychological tests) a music therapy prodecure could be set up where children are helped to learn to identify and to recall the sounds of musical instruments, arranged in sequences from one or two sounds up to four sounds. Periodic retesting with a psychological test of auditory memory would give indicators of progress and generalization to auditory memory for words and other sounds (Gregory, 1970).

An important aspect of music in special education where the expertise of the music therapist might be applied is in the whole area of speech and language. (A special section of this chapter will be devoted to this most important area of music therapy, but an example of a language stimulation project using music therapy is included here.)

Within a special education setting found in a training center or hospital for handicapped persons, a special program of music therapy — to develop not only improved speech but the use of appropriate language — might be set up. Here the music therapist might use several approaches to stimulate the use of appropriate language and increased conversation among individuals. Songs to identify and recognize by name the individuals in the group, songs to identify objects in the person's daily environment, and audio-visual materials stimulating the naming of objects and the use of these names, would be some of the approaches. In addition, the reward value of music might be used, that is, the increased efforts of individuals to make use of functional language (as well as appropriate use of certain words) would be rewarded by allowing the individuals to participate in their favorite form of music, whether listening to favorite recordings or learning simple instruments. Of course, measurements of progress would be taken at intervals by the music therapist (Walker, 1972).

This use of the reward value of music has very important implications for the use of music therapy in special education. Where, for example, a high prestige value exists for particular kinds of music activity for a group of children, these activities may be used to reinforce desirable learning activity in them. For special education children at a teenage level, for example a special education class in a junior high school, playing guitar might have high prestige value. Establishing group guitar lessons might be based upon the requirement of completing daily workbook assignments in the academic area. In this case, individuals would be required to earn points which would give them the privilege of taking part in the guitar instruction. Research already has indicated that such use of the reinforcing value of music activity can be reflected directly in academic achievement efforts of individual children ... and indeed, for a whole special education class (Michel, 1971).

PROBLEMS AND TREATMENT OF PHYSICALLY
HANDICAPPED CHILDREN

Children whose primary problem is considered to be physical may be handicapped as a result of birth defects, such as cerebral palsy, brain damage, debilitating disease (encephalitis, meningitis, poliomylitis), or disabling accidents.

What are the specific problems of physically handicapped children? Sensory disabilities such as vision (including the blind), hearing (including the deaf), speech and language disabilities (ranging from articulation to aphasia), and locomotion/coordination disabilities (from walking to eye-hand coordination), are the major problem areas. Specific problems under each category, ideally, are pinpointed for each individual — following the basic principle of therapy being individualized — and a program of remediation is devised, which frequently includes music therapy.

Let us not forget that most children will be multiply-handicapped in the true sense of the word, despite the fact that they may be classified or labelled under only one disability. (Sometimes the term "multi-handicapped" is used principally for those who have disabilities in two of the major areas listed above, e.g., deaf-blind, or speech and physical coordination.) Let us remember that social problems also prevail in nearly all cases. A person physically handicapped in any way is isolated to some degree from his peers, and this is bound to generate some social/emotional problems. Music therapy can make one of its most *important* and *unique* contributions in *this* area for nearly all physically handicapped children.

Visual Disabilities

What are some of the specific problems of visually handicapped children and how can music therapy be applied?

A landmark study of music therapy with the blind found music useful not only in helping blind persons learn rhythmic movement, so important in developing mobility skills (e.g., using a cane and learning to get around in one's environment independently), but also, in developing social skills (Unkefer, 1955). Blind persons need not all become musicians (or piano tuners) to benefit from music! They may, however, gain self-esteem in learning how to play the piano or guitar, or to sing and dance, and may also learn to use such skills in relating to others, individually and in groups. This is in addition to more specific treatment programs planned by a music therapist as in assisting a blind child in learning mobility skills by helping him move rhythmically to music.

A visually handicapped child has problems enough, deprived of one of the most important adaptive senses, but many visually handicapped children are also mentally retarded, or handicapped in other ways (multiply-handicapped). The music therapist often encounters such children, both in and out of institutions. What can he do for such a child?

If the child is retarded as well as blind, a music therapist may begin by determining what interests the child in music, and what music responses and abilities he already has. Does he like to listen to certain recordings? Does he like to play percussion instruments like jingle sticks, bells, or drums? Will he (can he) sing or hum? Will he move to musical rhythm? In other words, (a) what "turns him on" in music, and, (b) what can he do with music?

Perhaps even before assessing the child's musical interests and responses, or at least soon after, the therapist must find out what some of the child's basic and immediate problems are. If results of testing in social/emotional, or academic areas are present in his case file, the therapist must know this. Ultimately, the music therapist will want to do his own further assessment of specific problems of the child, in order to be able to set up treatment procedures i.e., the goals and objectives of music therapy, for this particular child.

As one example, the music therapist might first determine that one of the child's basic problems is in self-help skills, which prevents him from being able to participate in classroom activities. A specific problem may be in dressing himself. The therapist might devise a training program to teach the child how to go through the many steps of selecting and putting on pants, shirt, and shoes and socks. These steps might be sequenced by putting them into a song which the child could learn to sing while carrying out the steps involved. Singing along with the child, the therapist would take him through the step sequences at first: later, he would drop off the last step in the sequence and let the child "fill in" the missing link of behavior, cued by the song. Eventually, the song would be done only by the child himself, and, finally, the task completed without the song. If the child also was reinforced by favorite listening music, he might be given appropriate amounts of listening time as a reward, after completing specified amounts of work time on the problem. When a child has learned self-care behaviors such as those associated with dressing, he is ready for classroom association with other children, and further learning!

Since music exists in a time continuum, it is useful in many ways. One way this factor might be helpful with a blind, retarded child is in gaining his commitment to music participation through attention to music and expanding gradually his attending or on-task behavior in music, such as keeping time to the rhythm. This might be done by gradually increasing the demand for keeping time, and later, used to teach extended attention time to other academic or social learning tasks.

Another aspect of time in music, useful to blind children, is the rhythmic stimulation itself, which can be programmed to develop better physical coordination in the child, and even to help him develop mobility skills — getting around his environment as well as to learn control of large body movement (Clausell, 1974).

All visually handicapped children are not totally blind. Even "legal" blindness may leave a child with some residual or shadow vision, where he can distinguish some differences in light and dark, and "see" enough to be able to move around to some extent in his physical environment. Where does visual handicapping begin? Certainly any child who needs strong correction of vision may be considered handicapped. For such children, music therapy may offer means not only for structured learning of basic self-help and social skills, but may also provide helpful structures for learning basic academic skills such as auditory discrimination of words, counting, naming different sound cues, and imitation of sounds to learn how language is sequenced. While little research has yet been done, it is feasible that such uses of music might even be made to teach Braille reading for the visually handicapped child.

Another important use of music which has been reported quite often for the visually handicapped child is that of providing a compensatory device. If a blind child can learn to perform music, individually or in groups, he may have a means for easier social acceptance of sighted persons. In one public elementary school where there is a special education class for visually handicapped children, two teachers have organized a rhythm instrument and simple string band and the class performances are significant events. The applause and generous praise of those who "experience" the group no doubt makes a significant contribution to the self-concept and self-esteem of these children.

One possible negative aspect of this is the danger of music becoming the *only* means of compensatory benefit, i.e., where blind children may only grow up to become "blind musicians" or "blind piano tuners." Therapists must always take care not to over-emphasize the compensatory benefits of music for the visually handicapped, but to focus attention on the individual behind the music-making.

Finally, for *any* kind of therapy with the visually handicapped, it is important to recognize the individual rather than the disability or handicap. For example, not only are such children found within a range from partial vision loss to total blindness, they are also different in terms of the circumstances of their handicaps, i.e., it may be present at birth (congenital) or it may result from an injury (adventitious). In addition, the family or other environmental situation in which the child is found is a very important determinant of therapy. It may even be a factor for determining whether the therapist starts with treatment of problems of the handicap or with other problems, such as behavioral. A child has to first be able to attend to the therapist and the stimuli of therapy (music) before he can be helped.

Other potential benefits of music therapy are available to blind children: teaching cooperative and other social behaviors, such as in music groups where cooperation is demanded (a bell-choir group, for example, where each child must play a part of the melody with his assigned bell); or teaching socially accepted ways of expressing his feelings, through singing or playing instruments; or, teaching positive, constructive use of leisure time skills — listening to recorded music, learning to play an instrument, with the help of Braille (both words and music), the development of vocational or avocational skills in music.

Hearing Disabilities

Deaf? Hard of hearing? What is the difference? Both terms are relative and they describe similar conditions, but neither is really adequate. If we must attach a label to people with such disabilities, it is better to think of them as people with hearing losses, (just as it is better to think of people in the visual disability area as having loss of visual capacity). There is another difference that should be noted, and that is people who have become deaf for various reasons after they have once been able to hear, as contrasted with those who are born without hearing ability. For those who have never heard, a special problem exists with developing speech or any other kind of vocal sound-making behavior. Music therapy has a part to play in dealing with people who have lost hearing over a period of time for one reason or another, as well as with those who have never heard.

It is not only a way of helping people become aware of vibrations made by musical instruments or to perceive rhythm and rhythmic organization in music, but it is quite valuable as well in helping people become aware of areas (frequencies) of sound in which they may still be able to hear. Many people are only partially hard of hearing, and music, because of its wide range of frequencies employed, can be very useful in helping find the functioning area of frequency response. This may be expanded by the use of music as an attention-getting or attention-focusing stimulus to extend the client's awareness of other sounds as well as possibly helping him learn to use a hearing aid. The actual perception of music as sound vibration may be useful to some people in an organizing way. For example, if a child who is born deaf can become aware of the pulsations of music, and observes that there is a rhythmic regularity to it, that others are following this "beat," and that he may follow it also, this is the beginning of possible interactions of that individual with others in a social activity. In addition, it may be that the responsiveness to music pulses can be used as a way of helping the child develop rhythmic and meaningful expressive speech. Many deaf people, or people who have lost their hearing, lose a certain amount of vocal expressiveness, that is, the inflection and articulation of good speech. Of course, with those who are congenitally deaf, some aspects of speech have never developed. By encouraging people to emit vocal sounds in a rhythmic way (as in songs), it is possible to help them organize their speech into more interesting, meaningful patterns, and even to develop needed speech sounds themselves.

In one case, a student therapist working on campus in the speech pathology clinic found that she could help a pre-school child who was deaf become more attentive to her so that she could visually teach him other needed behaviors. She found that the interest of the child in rhythm instruments enabled her to set up a contingency system whereby when the child paid attention to her, he would be rewarded by being able to play a short time on the instruments. This procedure was used to expand the child's attention to the point where he was better able to accept other instruction.

In another case, a group of hearing-impaired children who had been deprived of earlier learning experiences because of their defect had to learn about the whole world of sound when they finally were fitted with hearing aids. Since much of our orientation to sounds is related to pitch discrimination, that is, to "high" and "low" sounds, such children must be taught to recognize the differences. Their learning to speak or to improve their present speech depends to a considerable extent on their recognition of high and low pitch concepts. Because of the unique and penetrating quality of some musical instruments and the possibility of their being played at wider pitch extremes than possible with human voices, one music therapy student used her clarinet to teach these children to recognize pitch differences, i.e., "high" and "low." Such pitch differences are, of course, important in every-day sound signals, such as horns and sirens.

Hearing disorders are not always detected and treated in

childhood. The author knows of cases of adults who grew up in an institution for the retarded who later became patients in a large state mental hospital, and who were essentially deaf, but *may* have been adjudged "retarded" and/or mute because of their deafness. In the state hospital their hearing loss was discovered — but how does one compensate for a lifetime lack of aural stimulation, a deprivation from the world of sound and the information it carries? A music therapist did succeed in orienting one of these persons, "J," to sound through headphone listening to rhythmic music. "J" showed such enthusiastic response to this new experience that it became something he would work very hard for, so it became a reward, a contingency for doing other assigned work/ learning tasks, such as learning to count. In addition, "J" learned to respond to the rhythm of rock music by playing on a set of trap drums along with recordings he "heard" through headphones. Before long, he could join others in such responses, and was socially accepted by them. Ultimately, "J's" discovery of rhythmic (musical) sound led to the beginning of his emitting vocal sounds, which eventually might evolve into elemental speech.

In Holland, Brother Leobert Gerits, following work done by Van Uden, Rutten, Groen, and others, after World War II, has developed several interesting techniques using music and dance to train severely deaf children in sound perception and the development of language. Beginning with "Home Training" for pre-school children, training parents to help their children learn lip-reading and the use of hearing aids, the program of the Saint Michielsgestel Institute employs numerous techniques to help deaf children change from being "eye-persons" to being more sound- and vibration-oriented (Gerits, 1967).

Methods used include expressive movements and dance as response to rhythmic sound vibrations of music; experience in creating sounds on various instruments like drums, melodicas, and a specially constructed "blow organ;" and the use of melody to teach speech patterns and inflection. Vibrating response depends upon the children's perceiving sound through various resonating cavities of their bodies rather than through bone conduction (hands, feet) since (it is wisely noted), contact with the pulse of sound is lost when the child lifts a foot while dancing, or removes a hand from the vibrating source, such as a loudspeaker.

The principle of gaining awareness and control of sound through feedback mechanisms when a child produces his own sounds (musical instruments, vocal) is emphasized. Such exercises, e.g., using the "blow organ," are also structured for improving breath control for vocal sounds, self-produced.

While this work has not yet been reported in scientific terms, i.e., accurate measurements of results, the principles seem very sound and worthy of research by music and speech therapists.

To summarize, the use of music therapy for the deaf can be described in four basic ways: (1) the use of vibration, especially the organized vibrations of music to gain and expand attention; (2) the use of music and its wide range of frequencies to assist in the diagnosis of hearing loss and development of hearing potential; (3) the use of the rhythmic pulsation of music to help develop social relationships in movement with others, such as in a dance or instrumental group activity (rhythm bands); and (4) to regulate speech mechanisms in the development of language, i.e., in learning discriminations of pitch range (high and low), or in rhythmic patterning and pitch inflections of speech.

Gross and Sensory Motor Disabilities

Physical disabilities resulting in problems of locomotion and coordination arise from a large variety of sources and causes. A child may be crippled at birth by difficulties during the birth itself, or by prenatal conditions, such as disease, or accident. The crippled child may be physically unable to develop the necessary bone and muscle combinations to learn to walk at the normal time. Or, he may have physical problems, such as deformed limbs that make locomotion (walking) at best a long, hard process.

Diseases of childhood may leave a child physically disabled. Poliomyelitis became rare in the USA in the 1960's after the widespread innoculations of the Salk vaccine. But in the 1970's concern developed for a possible renewed outbreak of the disease and its crippling effects as individuals and public health facilities seemed to grow lax and complacent about requiring innoculation. Besides "polio" (sometimes called infantile paralysis), other diseases are crippling, especially forms of disease which attack brain or central nervous system tissue, such as encephalitis and meningitis. Since central nervous system tissues (brain and spinal cord) do not regenerate or heal and replace themselves, crippling effects are usually permanent.

One of the crippling conditions found at birth is *cerebral palsy (C-P)*. This is a condition often resulting from birth difficulties, e.g., "breach birth," which deprives the infant's brain of sufficient oxygen, culminating in physical disability of varying severity, ranging from almost total paralysis to mild symptoms of muscular discoordination. In a sense C-P is a form of brain damage, since brain tissue is destroyed (from insufficient oxygen). The term "brain damage" however, is usually applied in cases where specific injury or disease has damaged the brain.

Accidents, especially those involving children and automobiles, often result in permanent physical disabilities in locomotion and coordination. The specific disabilities may be the result of loss or permanent damage to limbs, or to the central nervous system, affecting the movement of limbs. The disablement may be very similar to that found as a result of birth defects or crippling diseases.

Treatment of physically handicapped children, especially those with coordination and locomotion problems, may begin in a special rehabilitation center such as those sponsored by the Easter Seal Society or by United Cerebral Palsy. On the other hand, many such children are treated in hospitals and centers for the "retarded." (It may be, in many cases a simple matter of economic or social condition of families of such children, where they will be found. Those children cared for by their families and taken to community centers for treatment will generally do better. Home reinforcement of clinic treatment is invaluable!)

What can music therapy offer to children with these problems of coordination and locomotion? The use of music to stimulate, accompany, and regulate physical movement is one of the most primitive functions of music for man. The potential for its application with crippled children lies in these functions. Background music, appropriately chosen by a music therapist, may assist the physical or occupational therapist working with the stiffened limbs of a child by helping the child feel relaxed and cooperative. Music extemporized by the music therapist, e.g., playing the piano, can stimulate the therapeutic movements needed to gain coordination in the child when he is able to initiate movement himself. Music can also influence by its rhythm and tempo, the movement of a child *at his level of potentiality.* With carefully timed segments, it can regulate the amounts of exercise desirable. Physical and occupational therapists may expect a music therapist to be able to provide "treatment packages" appropriate to the needs and capabilities of individual patients. When children are ready for common involvement in a group (which may be fairly early in their treatment, since many varieties and levels of response to music are available in the same selection), they can incorporate the stimulation of music with the stimulation of the group, in a manner *especially unique to music therapy.*

An example of one way music therapy is applied in these areas is the six-year-old crippled child found in a hospital for the mentally retarded. "Dicky" did not walk, but physical therapists advised that, at that point, he could probably learn to walk if sufficiently motivated. A music therapist began to work with him and found that he liked music and enjoyed moving his hands and arms while music was played. He especially liked the smooth rhythm of Strauss waltzes. Playing waltz music recordings, and with the assistance of a modified tricycle which allowed "Dicky" to pedal without going anywhere, the music therapist helped him begin to strengthen his leg muscles. Gradually increasing the demands by playing the music for longer intervals, the therapist helped him reach a level of strength and confidence where he could take his first walking steps — still supported by Strauss waltz music.

Another example with an older child found a music therapist using music to help a brain-injured teenage girl to regain finger strength and coordination by learning to play the organ. The goal was to give her needed exercise to regain digital and hand control, necessary in self-help skills such as dressing and eating, as well as in academic skills requiring writing. At the same time, learning a music performance skill was aimed at giving the young lady a source of self-esteem which might help her to be more constructive in her social relationships than with her behaviors of complaining and attempting to "manipulate" hospital employees. Music therapy did help her to make progress in these ways, and is playing a part in her further rehabilitation today, as she learns to sing and to join in group activities.

Speech Disorders and Disabilities

That there is a close relationship between speech therapy and music therapy has been observed for a long time. In recent work, one can see more precisely what contributions each field can make toward the other, and more importantly, how therapists in both fields can work together cooperatively, toward a more effective treatment of many patients with speech and hearing disorders (Seybold, 1971). Where there are no qualified therapists from either one of these two disciplines, the one present certainly can benefit greatly by "borrowing" techniques from the other field. The following studies illustrate some of both of these kinds of situations (Michel, May, 1974).

They have ranged from fairly broad-spectrum problems, such as the use of music stimuli in teaching language discrimination, to rather minute ones, such as the use of music as an aid in teaching specific consonants to speech handicapped children. It has been fortunate that such close cooperation has existed between speech pathologists, hearing specialists, and music therapists both at the Florida State University and in the community of Tallahassee and Leon County, Florida, which has made it possible not only to conduct these studies but also to replicate and improve upon them. In one study, an interdisciplinary approach was made possible through a University research grant, where professors from music education, psychology, and music therapy collaborated. In another instance, three students in a graduate music therapy class, representing speech pathology, and music therapy in two different settings, were able to collaborate on a study, testing out a common methodology in three different settings.

Methodology varied from the case study approach with

individuals and small groups to carefully controlled statistical designs, using several groups of subjects. Several examples of methods and procedures, as well as examples of evaluation techniques will follow.

An example of a student project which made use of a group approach in music to accomplish several stated goals was one done by Stadsklev (1966). In this study, a common procedural model of the mid-sixties years was followed, i.e., the case study. Stadsklev and the teacher of a class of cerebral-palsied children evaluated the project through case-study descriptions. The results of seven 45-minute weekly music sessions were reported as: "noticeable improvement" in speech, muscle coordination, self-expression, and socialization for all of the children.

Studies done by several students one year later also followed the case-study model, but with increasing attempts to measure in more concrete ways the results of treatment. Students Davis, Slonin, Walker, (unpublished, 1967) and others worked with individuals in the annual summer residential speech and hearing clinic, held on the FSU campus.

Slonin reported results from music therapy sessions with a seven-year old boy who had a severe hearing loss, which were: development of a six-note singing range (from no range), ability to match six random pitches, ability to sing three familiar folk songs with acceptable articulation of the words, ability to respond appropriately to rhythm in music, and ability to play simple chords on autoharp for familiar songs.

Davis found music helpful with a fifteen-year-old deaf girl, especially in her socialization with a group where she learned to interact through perceiving the rhythm and its response in others (visually) and by becoming aware of the vibrations of the music used.

Walker worked with a twelve-year-old boy who had a partial hearing loss. Music therapy goals of improved vocal production (inflection, voice projection) and in following directions for playing instruments like the autoharp; increasing attention span, and developing better physical coordination through rhythmic responses to music, were judged to have been achieved. The most dramatic behavior change attributed to the music however, was that this formerly non-socializing boy was, at the end of the clinic, playing autoharp accompaniments for the other children's singing!

In the summer of 1968, a more sophisticated study concerning language development problems of disadvantaged pre-school children, was conducted by an interdisciplinary team. Music therapy, music education, and psychology were the disciplines involved in exploring the problems of auditory language discrimination in 216 Head Start children. It found generally that practice *songs* (for word discriminations) and tonal cues paired with words were significantly more effective than four other conventional and innovative methods of training (Madsen, Michel, Madsen, 1975).

One replication of the auditory language discrimination study was done by a graduate music therapy student working with cleft-palate children. Irwin found that among twenty cleft-palate children, those who were "treated" with stories which used the test words (sound-blends), and those treated with these stories set to music, significantly improved over other children given more conventional speech therapy. There were only five treatment sessions used for each group in the experiment. The Songs Group improved the most, the Stories Group second, and both significantly improved over other experimental groups and from pre- to post-measurement periods (1969).

Language development along with speech therapy has been the focus of several studies, including one masters thesis. One study, done by three graduate students using the same methodology (basically, special songs) with three different groups of retardates in three different settings, used "operant" methods of evaluation, such as graphed comparisons of changes, from pre- to post-evaluation points. The results were interpreted as positive, i.e., indicating that the children had learned and improved specifically the use of *r* and *s* sounds in their speech, through music therapy procedures (Irwin, Plumb, Walker, 1971) (See also Walker, 1972).

Research which utilized specially composed music to gain improved articulation by a group of disadvantaged Negro children was done by Marsh. Focusing on the ending *s* sounds, such as those found in the *Pledge of Allegiance to the Flag*, Marsh used the song form for one group in comparison with rhythmic chanting for another and with a third no-contact control group, to determine which method might be effective for children who had no ending *s* sounds in several words in the *Pledge of Allegiance*. The unique aspect of this research was in its use of sound spectographic equipment to analyze the speech sounds in question. While the findings were not statistically significant, strong trends were evident that the song group had made improvement, i.e., improved *s* sounds from a pretreatment level of only 53% of all subjects making correct articulation of *one* s-consonant to 90% making one or more correct articulations of *s* after treatment (Marsh, Fitch, 1970).

Two other programs have further demonstrated the important contribution of music therapy for people with speech and language problems. One was done as part of a summer research and demonstration project at an Easter Seal Rehabilitation Center. Six children were individually referred to the music therapist by the speech therapist. Problems varied from the need to elicit speech from a cerebral-palsied child to problems of auditory discrimination, short attention span, eye-hand coordination, and the development of simple language patterns. Sessions varied from seven to twenty-two for each child, and results, scientifically evaluated by various means, were "highly positive" or "positive" (significant) in six instances, mildly positive in two, and negative in only one behavior (the six children exhibited more than one problem "behavior" each), (Greenfield, 1971).

Another part of the project dealt with three children referred from a language development class being conducted at the center. Here again, positive results were measured after only 17 - 20 sessions. Over all, it seemed obvious that music therapy was not just a supplement to speech therapy and language development, but that specific, unique contributions were made through music therapy.

Working closely with speech and hearing professional staff therapists, two students proceeded along a well-planned course toward achieving speech improvement goals through music therapy. These ranged from appropriate attending behavior in a classroom setting to specific procedures to extend pitch range, increase duration of vocal loudness, and improve pitch discrimination and matching abilities. With the assistance of speech and hearing therapy students working along with the groups of children, speech therapy goals were further interlaced with the music sessions by the speech therapy students observing and rewarding positive efforts of individual children during the music therapy sessions. ("Positive efforts" were those corresponding with the speech therapy prescription for each child, which was revised weekly.) Although the effects of this sort of cooperative interdisciplinary approach are difficult to evaluate, or to assign to a single variable such as music, the end results for each child were undeniably improvement. Post-test comparisons with pre-test items concerning the strictly musical aspects such as increased loudness and pitch-matching left no doubt about the specific effectiveness of the music therapy sessions, however (Wilson, Hendrick, 1971).

Accumulated experience and scientific study of the use of music therapy in speech, language and hearing disorders, indicate a gradual refinement of procedures, and more sophisticated evaluation of results. There is growing support for the opinion that music therapy is not only an additional modality adjunctive to speech pathology, but that there are unique contributions to be made — both independently and in interdisciplinary ways, by music therapy in the treatment of persons with such disorders.

PROBLEMS AND TREATMENT OF CHILDREN AND ADOLESCENTS WITH BEHAVIORAL DISORDERS

General Considerations

Children who have behavioral disorders are grouped here with adolescents, not because the disorders are exactly the same, but because they have similar origins, i.e., in the developmental process of growing up. Adult disorders tend to be more complex, usually having developed over a longer period of time, and are more likely to be associated with stresses of every-day adaptation, either as an acute reaction to crises or a more chronic reaction resulting from distress over a longer period of time.

The problems of childhood and adolescence are no less serious than those of adulthood, but they are more likely to be related to transitory factors of growth and development. Thus one must look to the patterns of growth and development all persons experience in childhood and adolescence to observe where the problems are likely to occur, and where disorders may originate. Human beings, while infinitely unique, are at the same time uniquely alike in many ways, and their problems which arise from unsatisfactory adaptations — to themselves or to the society in which they live — are remarkably similar. Behavioral problems experienced in childhood and adolescence, whether or not considered a full-blown "disorder," may arise from difficulties or deficiencies of a child in performing self-help skills; in paying attention long enough to sustain learning; in developing adequate language and speech; in developing satisfactory gross-motor and fine-motor coordination; or in perceptual-motor skills such as eye-hand coordination.

Problems might arise in social-adaptive areas such as learning how to cooperate with others, or in physical and verbal interaction (social patterns) with others. The learning of basic educative skills such as the traditional Three R's is the source of behavioral maladaptations for some.

In the first ten years or so of life, when self-concept or self-image is developing, problems may arise to become behavior disorders. Self-esteem is considered to be one of the most important aspects of human development, and is subject to considerable stress as a child expands his contacts with the world, especially in interactions with others (social).

If problems are specific to such contacts with others, but not so much related to self-concept, they might be considered "social-adaptive" rather than self-esteem problems. Social-adaptive problems are especially important in adolescence as individuals begin to enter the adult world. Not only are they confronted with the problems which are brought on by the physical changes of puberty, but, also, in many societies, they are expected to be loyal members of their peer group while at the same time they are being "initiated" into adulthood, or giving up peer group influence to become independent, responsible adults.

Perhaps at this point a differentiation needs to be made between problems and disorders. "Behavior disorder" generally refers to a pattern of handicapping problems, or a major single problem which has escalated into *distress,* then become a *disorder.* Behavioral therapists generally approach treatment by attempting to isolate specific problems or problem-behaviors with which they may work, in the hope that the overall adaptation of the individual will be improved. (Perhaps it is more fair to say that behavior therapists *define* the disorder in terms of the "symptoms," or individual, specific behavior problems.)

Therapists working under other therapy orientations such as those derived from psychoanalysis, may use labels which describe behavior disorders in more general terms, e.g., *neurosis.* While it is not within the scope of this book to go into detail concerning theoretical bases of different therapy orientations, it is the author's preference to consider disorders in the behaviorist orientation, i.e., as a set of (or sometimes only one) problem-behaviors which cause the individual to be impaired in adaptation — to himself and/or his environment. As indicated above, there may be more to it than this, but beginning with identification of specific problem-behaviors seems a good place to start.

In such an orientation, it is interesting to note that many of the problem-behaviors are the same as, or similar to, those described earlier for other client populations, such as retarded and physically handicapped. The concept of multiply-handicapped also applies to those whose primary designation is behavior disorder. The disorder may be found in combination with other problems — not only in disease or disability categories, but also overflowing into physiological problem areas. The somewhat hazy area of interplay of disorder with bodily function is known as psychosomatic medicine. In the disability areas: physical, developmental (the newer term encompassing mental retardation), and learning, problems may well be primarily behavioral; or, disability problems may be accompanied by or result in behavioral problems.

Behavioral disorders not only arise from stress in disease, disability, and social interaction areas, they may also be by-products of the social/economic environment in which the child lives. Deprivation in terms of economic, social, or education opportunities is now being recognized as an important factor underlying the development of behavioral disorders. Disadvantaged children in an inner city ghetto would certainly seem to be more susceptible to problems of behavior when they move into other segments of the community. Racial and other discrimination biases in themselves may be a part of the disadvantagement and deprivation facing some children in our society, and may lead to increased incidence of problem behaviors. It should also be noted that deprivation and disadvantagement is not limited to inner city ghettos; it can occur in rural proverty areas, and even within an "impoverished" family, when impoverishment includes a lack of adequate stimulation (and perhaps the deadening effect of television or other constant, noisy stimuli?).

What can music therapy contribute to the treatment of behaviorally disordered children and adolescents? How can it contribute? When one confronts the variety of problems and problem situations in which disorders may be found (not to mention the labyrinth of labels and terms used to describe the disorders), it may seem at first to be hopelessly confusing. The recognition of the common denominator of *problem-behaviors* and the focus upon attempting to change such behaviors should be helpful. Even such perplexing disorders as early infantile autism may be better understood and dealt with when specific behaviors are studied and are made the target of therapeutic effort. (The term early infantile autism, it was noted, infers a disorder which might possibly be in the disease or disability category; however, so far, research has not found developmental or bacterial/viral causal factors. The relatively low incidence of cases meeting the criteria some have established to warrant a child's being put into the EIA category, makes it a matter worthy of only limited attention. However, the *behaviors* ascribed to such children have been called autistic, and this term has seemed to expand in usage, so that now many children are given the label "autistic.")

Examples of Music Therapy

A music therapist, confronted with a child labelled "autistic" would first want (under a behavioral therapy orientation) to observe behaviors of such a child over a period of time, so that he might target one or two problem behaviors he might try to change. In the process of observing behaviors of the child in different circumstances, the music therapist would wish to determine, if possible, what music the child responds to and what musical responses (to rhythm, melody, etc.) he might have. This information would be critical for planning therapy through music.

Since *some* children who are essentially retarded also exhibit "autistic-like" behaviors, e.g., spinning around, or repetitive-ritualistic hand movements, it would be important to ascertain whether or not the child was primarily autistic or retarded. However, for immediate treatment, approaches might be similar. One factor which could possibly assist in differential diagnosis might be the child's reaction and responses to music. The autistic child probably would exhibit more sophisticated responses, such as initiating fairly complex rhythmic and melodic patterns, or in manipulating a phonograph. A retarded child most likely would not exhibit such responses with any sophistication.

If the behavior problem which is focused upon is one of isolation or alienation of the child from persons in the environment, i.e., he does not respond to normal approaches of therapists, nurses, etc., and if the child has shown some responsiveness to music such as attending to recorded music, showing curiosity in manipulating a phonograph or simple rhythm instruments, a program of therapy could be started in which the interest in music could be used to draw the child into contact with the therapist. For example, the music therapist, controlling recorded music (or instruments) could systematically reward the child when he was physically close to the therapist, and/or showed any signs of communication by reinforcing with the music, AND COULD WITHHOLD the music when inappropriate or inadequate responses were made by the child. The goal would be increasing the frequency of physical "closeness" of the child with the therapist and stimulating the child to communicate, either through involvement in music at the non-verbal level, or in other interactive ways, including verbal (Bosco, 1974).

One theory of music therapy for approaching withdrawn,

non-communicative, "autistic" children which has so far received much attention but little scientific validation, relies on the principle of trying to meet the child where he is, in terms of matching his movements and imitating them in music improvised by the therapist. A child's inadvertent or accidental sound-making, or his movement about in a room, might be considered a form of music-making which is incorporated by the therapist into a music structure, extended, and fed back immediately to the child in an effort to get him to repeat the original behavior (or otherwise respond), and thus to begin to complete a communication "circuit" with the therapist. This approach offers a real challenge, both musically and therapeutically, for the therapist and deserves careful evaluation in terms of scientific measurement. Such creative music-making approaches have long been advocated and used in music education as a means of getting children to begin music-making experience, letting it develop or reflect, as it were, from the child's actual behaviors (Nordoff and Robbins, 1971).

If music therapists can help autistic children increase communicative contact with others, such children have a better chance of entering the mainstream of education. While experimental research supporting this function of music therapy is still sparse, there are many case examples reported which strongly indicate music therapy does have an important part to play with treatment of such children.

How can therapy through music contribute to children and adolescents with other behavior disorders? An earlier part of this chapter provided examples of how music therapy functions in special education settings in the schools, in terms of children with problems in learning, auditory memory, and other pre-reading/language skills, and self-esteem. Further examples of music therapy with visual, auditory, and locomotion problems were also provided, along with examples of music in speech therapy. Some of these applications and approaches may apply to children whose *behavior disorder* problems are similar, e.g., speech and language problems.

Outside of school special education programs, behavior-disordered children may be found in hospitals (more and more special facilities for severely disturbed, behavior-disordered children are being provided within, *and* separate from state mental hospitals), in special schools, and in community clinics and centers. Where they are found depends more upon social-economic factors than differential diagnosis of their disorders, as has been noted in the case with children whose problems are centered in retardation. A music therapist can work in any of these settings, and as he focuses on specific problems, treatment through music may follow similar patterns. Using the structuring aspect of music to organize learning, the reinforcing (reward) aspect to help change old behavioral patterns and shape new ones, or the social group aspect to develop interpersonal interaction and to structure appropriate involvement of individuals in social settings, the music therapist tends to work in much the same general way, whatever the problem or behavior disorder.

Besides working with communication problems (attention, interaction, language, speech, etc.), and self-esteem problems, music therapists may encounter in children with behavior disorders problems in self-expression, e.g., inappropriate reactions to requests for cooperation with others. Musical tools, both as reinforcers, and as structure, as in group activity, may be applied to help children with such problems learn better ways of reacting to and dealing with self-expression, as well as with social interaction problems. Music study and performance itself may provide avenues of self-expression (sometimes delayed in time from the frustrating stimulus), as well as a useful, *constructive* activity for leisure-time. Music skills at many levels provide many persons in any society with pleasurable, leisure-time activity.

PROBLEMS AND TREATMENT OF "DELINQUENT" CHILDREN AND ADOLESCENTS

Who is a Delinquent?

The stereotype of a juvenile delinquent for most people is the teenage youth, usually male, who has run afoul of the law or is on the fringes of law-breaking. He is a child who has become delinquent in his obedience to the law, or in his general behavior with regard to those rules and conventions of institutions and society that most people follow. He (or she) often has gone beyond the regular mechanisms of a school or other institution in society for regulating his behavior. His (her) behavior may have been labeled by teachers, counselors, or principals as:

—unmanageable	—unpredictable
—intransigent	—hyperactive
—intractible	—aggressive
—recalcitrant	—destructive
—chronic offender	—hostile
—incorrigible	—or even as "dangerous" to others and himself,

or he might be labeled simply as "truant," i.e., frequently absent from school.

At a more severe stage, the juvenile delinquent has been arrested by an officer of the law for a variety of possible offenses, from illegal possession of drugs (a major problem in recent years, which will be discussed in more detail later), to "breaking and entering" and acts of physical violence toward others. The youthful lawbreaker in our society usually is accorded special treatment under the laws of most states and the Federal Government, so that he is referred to a special court or other authority, as in Florida, where a state division of youth services provides a network of detention centers and counselors.

What criteria are used to decide that there is to be "special treatment" for juvenile offenders? *Age* is the most important factor — in most states any child up to age seventeen is considered a "juvenile" for special consideration. Since national suffrage (voting rights) has been granted to eighteen-year-olds, there seems to be a trend toward more stringent treatment of older teenagers by courts of law. Other criteria generally are: the nature of the unlawful act — i.e., its severity (murder, other physical violence), and repetitions of "brushes" with the law. Chronic offenders may ultimately be dealt with by the regular courts of law.

One other factor must be mentioned: the distinction between "delinquent" and "dependent" categories of young persons in homeless by tragedy often becomes the concern of juvenile authorities and is given special treatment. Sometimes there may be a fine line of demarcation between delinquent and dependent, where the hitch-hiking runaway breaks laws of vagrancy, loitering, or even laws against hitch-hiking, in some locales. The dependent child is offered the protection of a special court or other authority, which acts for him as the representative of society. Ideally, such authority sometimes becomes viewed as protector or advocate of delinquent children, as was the case with one young man who was counseled by the author while working as a volunteer counselor for a juvenile court.

What Can Music Therapy Do?

In one of the author's experiences, music became the medium of "reconciliation" between him and "Tommy," the young man assigned to him by the juvenile court. The counselor's role represents to many youths that of another officer of the court, a representative of the law. In truth, this is the counselor's official position, but he also represents the advocate position of the law, i.e., *for* the youth. To convince a young, belligerent boy of this, however, is another matter.

Tommy got into trouble through truancy. The author was assigned to work with him after he had been caught several times away from school when he was supposed to be there. At the first hearing by a juvenile judge, local welfare people were also present to report on a continuing investigation which had been going on regarding the condition of the boy's home — whether or not it was suitable for him to continue to live in, i.e., whether or not minimum health standards were maintained by his mother, the only parent. In other words, the question was raised as to whether or not he should be declared a *dependent* child and made a ward of the court for possible foster home placement.

At the same time, Tommy had become a "delinquent" through his persistent truancy (and his being seen with a gang of boys, some of whom were already in "fringe" trouble with the law). The decision of the court was to assign Tommy to the author for counseling, as a delinquent, not a dependent.

At the first session, basic ground rules were set up by the counselor, such as regular attendance at school, and weekly meetings with the counselor. The counselor's identity as a music therapy professor who was volunteering as a counselor led Tommy to disclose his interest in music, mainly recordings, and his interest in learning to play guitar. It did not lead immediately to Tommy's relinquishing his basic distrust of the counselor and his visible hostility toward him, however.

After two counseling meetings, the counselor offered to teach Tommy how to play guitar. Tommy would "earn" guitar lessons if he could report weekly not only regular attendance in school, but also evidence of completing schoolwork, validated by his teachers. (He was then age fifteen, in the tenth grade.) Since Tommy had no guitar, an offer was made for him to "earn" the guitar over a period of time by the same rules, plus showing progress in guitar performance weekly. (The guitar was purchased through donations by friends of the counselor.)

Before long, Tommy's proverty-striken mother somehow arranged to buy him his own guitar — perhaps out of a sense of pride. Lessons continued, sessions continued, and Tommy stayed in school and passed all his subjects. This is not the end of Tommy's story, however. That story continues over a period of years when the counselor's role finally evolved to that of friend, after Tommy was released from the court's jurisdiction. Although not measureable in concrete terms, it is the author's opinion that the guitar lessons helped Tommy overcome his hostility toward the counselor, and generally, toward the law. In one episode later, when Tommy was in the Job Corps, he made a firm decision to identify *with* the law, rather than against it, when opportunity was provided to do otherwise.

Subsequently, Tommy enlisted in the Army, finished high-school-equivalency work, learned basic clerical skills, and returned from the Army back into society, apparently with good adaptation.

Other examples of the application of music therapy show somewhat more specifically some techniques employed. One such instance found music being used as a contingency for desired behavior of a young man who had been put under the court's jurisdiction because of his violence and threatened violence, particularly towards his mother (who found him to be "incorrigible"). The volunteer counselor, (a colleague of the author), following a behavioral model, set stringent rules for the boy to follow in his interactions with his mother. This included appropriate verbalizations, and was to be monitored by the mother who would report to the counselor. Again, guitar lessons were offered (when an interest had been expressed by the boy) as a reward for following the rules set down by the counselor. The counselor, however, had no illusions about the rules being followed so easily and maintained a vigil over the home until he observed what he had expected — a reversion to old behavior patterns by the young man, whereupon the counselor administered "aversive verbal reinforcement" (scolded and threatened him), and gave him a rough board out of which he was to fashion a heavy paddle. The paddle was to be used if the mother reported the son's breaking the basic rules, and it was to be brought for inspection to each counseling session. Progress on the construction of the paddle also became a part of the contingency for guitar lessons. The violent behavior soon extinguished, the paddle was never used, and the young man continued to study guitar, even after dismissal from the counselor's jurisdiction (Madsen & Madsen, 1968).

Another use of music as a facilitator is possible in the area of self-esteem or self-concept. Early studies in this area have shown that self-esteem, as measured by self-rating and teacher-rating, can be raised in boys who were labelled "problem behavior" or delinquent. The learning of simple music skills, such as playing chords on the ukulele to accompany simple, social songs, was the facilitative role of music. In this study, it is important to note that the music therapists were concerned about *measuring* the effects of music study upon self-esteem, as well as whether or not self-esteem itself was a factor in the problems evidenced by the boys, and whether or not a change in self-esteem generalized to improved behavior of the boys (which in this instance, it did) (Michel & Farrell, 1973).

So often in considering juvenile delinquency, it seems that only males suffer this label. For those persons teaching in junior high schools, middle schools, and high schools, however, the fallacy of this assumption is often demonstrated. In one public middle school setting, a music therapist used music as a facilitator for improvement of social behaviors among a group of boys *and* girls who had been designated by school authorities as problem behavior children.

Treatment sessions were structured so that one period every day at mid-day was a music listening hour for these children. The hour was under the supervision of the music therapist, who established the basic rules of social behaviors and interaction to be followed among the children, and whose only contingency was control of the recorded music to be played on the hi-fi set. (Choice of music was that of the group.) Her contingency was that whenever any individual in the group broke or failed to observe one of the rules, the music would stop, and be interrupted for a period of time. Thus, both group *and* music were put into play as facilitators for desired group/individual behavior.

Over a period of only a few weeks, all the boys and girls in the group were receiving their music listening privilege almost continuously throughout the hour, and their improved social behaviors were being reported as reflected in other classrooms. This seemed to demonstrate the powerful reinforcing value of music (plus peer group influence) on behaviors of these teenagers (Hanser, 1972).

Delinquent acts which put young persons under closer supervision than assignment to a counselor or a special remedial group in school, may result in their being placed into one of a variety of detention and "correctional" or "training" settings. These range from temporary detention centers through longer-term confinement institutions to half-way houses near or in communities, where young offenders may live in a supervised group setting and may go to school and otherwise interact in the community. At such a place, trained counselors may use group therapy and other treatment methods with the young inmates. In any type of setting, music therapy may have a place.

Music is a natural group facilitator. Think of the many activities in music which are group-oriented: dances, choruses, combos, and instrumental groups of various kinds! If a music therapist is part of the staff in detention centers, where the length of detention is relatively short (from one to three weeks, usually), group music therapy may be used to help persons regain poise and to feel more at ease with other inmates as well as with staff members. Group listening to recordings, group singing, group playing of simple percussion-type instruments, and group movement to music, all may serve to reassure inmates, to help them relax, to give them a means for release of tensions and anxieties, and possibly to influence a more positive attitude about their confinement, whatever the reason for it may be.

A music therapy student project to explore potentials for music therapy in a county detention center (A Survey, 1966) found many possibilities for the use of music, not only in group situations, but also in stimulating the interest of individuals in a new activity which might be pursued once they left the center. A music therapist in the community might work with individuals, as well as with groups (see preceding description of the case of Tommy).

The music therapist should be able to provide his clients, whether they be referrals from juvenile authorities or from other sources, with entry to the musical life of the community. More will be said about how this can be done later, but at this point, it should be noted that most communities today have few activities in music for interested persons.

In a half-way house setting, music therapy has a definite potential role. In one place known to the author, a half-way house for boys centers its treatment program around "reality therapy," which is a form of group therapy with each individual expected to interact, and to be as honest with himself as possible, as well as with others. Group control is a large factor, residing in the group itself, with counselors (ideally) limited to guidance and suggestion. The decisions for individual privileges, as well as even for individual treatment programs are made by the group most of the time, after open discussion (Glasser, 1965).

In such a program, music therapy in the form of instruction on guitar or other musical instruments could be designated as a privilege earned by an individual boy, and at the same time, could be a part of his treatment, e.g., if he pursued lessons faithfully and consistently and gained an important new leisure-time skill, or perhaps, even avocational skill, such as developing into a competent bandsman in a part-time commercial combo. Music also might be introduced into group meetings in the form of record-listening, using recordings of popular songs or movie themes which could stimulate specific topics for discussion, i.e., topics of importance to the group therapeutic process. If developing group spirit and closeness and loyalty is a goal for the boys, music in the form of making and playing simple instruments is another possible application (if done under goals and direction of a music therapist). Of course, *specifying* treatment or learning goals for any client is a very important function.

Children and adolescents labelled delinquent or dependent in our society often are assigned to specially designated persons and places for help. Mild forms of problem behaviors in schools which are called delinquent may be treated by specialists, including music therapists, in school settings. Children and adolescents who get into trouble with law enforcement agencies and persons, may be assigned to special counselors within the community, may spend time in detention centers, may be required to spend time in more strictly controlled institutions such as correctional or training schools, or may be treated in community "half-way houses."

In each and all of these settings, music therapy may have an important role, whether or not a full-time music therapist is employed. In the community situations there is more likelihood that music therapists will be found in part-time assignments at several places. Also, music therapists may be expected to be liaison persons for helping individuals find extensions and applications of their music activities in the community, during and after treatment. There is a great challenge for music therapists to develop innovative and correlative programs in working with delinquency.

What about the more disturbing and sometimes related problems of children and adolescents who are drug abusers and drug addicts? Does music therapy have a contribution to make here?

DRUG ABUSE AND DEPENDENCY

We human beings believe in medicine. We have confidence for

the most part in medical doctors to help us get well, or to feel better, often with the assistance of drugs. Medicine available without doctors' prescriptions, sometimes known as "patent medicine," is one of the biggest industries of this country and of the world. Most of us depend to some extent on such medicine, from aspirin to liniment, to ease our pain at various times. Is it any wonder our children learn to *believe* in drugs? Besides patent medicines, many adults depend upon drugs like coffee, tea, tobacco, and alcohol to provide stimulation or relaxation at various moments in their lives. The problem of addictive drugs, mostly illegally procured, is one still wide-spread in our society, and in the world at large, not only in the toll it takes in human agony and lives, but even in terms of its related consequences in international relations.

Our society then, and its beliefs about the magic and miracles of drugs, is part of the problem when young people become drug abusers and drug dependents. (An intermediate stage is sometimes called drug "experimentation.") However, the basic problem is that of individual children and/or adolescents falling into one of the categories of drug usage which places them beyond the loosely defined "norms" of society, i.e., when they require treatment or become involved with the illegal use or possession of certain drugs.

Before dealing more specifically with music therapy's role in working with children/adolescents with drug abuse or dependency problems, it might be well to review briefly some definitions of drugs and the categories into which they fall. One listing which this author prefers gives four categories as follows: a) *Narcotics* = medically, anything which induces sleep or masks pain; legal definition: opiates such as heroin, codein, and morphine; b) *Sedatives* = medically, means barbiturates, tranquilizers, and alcohol; c) *Stimulants* = medically refers mostly to amphetamines; and d) *Hallucinogens* = refers mostly to LSD, marijuana, hashish, and other drugs which cause altered states of consciousness.

Early reports of music therapists working with youthful addicts included one from therapists at a state hospital in New Jersey. Here, adolescents who had been identified as having a drug problem, either through problems with the law or with medical or psychological problems attributable to drug abuse or addiction, were committed to the state hospital for treatment. Music therapists found that such patients did relate to them and that possibly this was due to a belief that music therapists could be trusted since they "understood" the kind of music (popular) that they did, and often spoke the same kind of language the patients did. (Much of the slang and jargon used by persons involved in drugs was also used by popular musicians.) The trusting relationship could sometimes be turned into an influential one, so that patients left the hospital with a belief in some of the "straight" people (music therapists), and that it was worthwhile to try to live without drugs, especially if you could get equally "turned on" to music as the music therapists were.

Much has been said and written about the possible cause-and-effect relationships of music and drugs, but so far, very little research has been reported. Undoubtedly, a considerable amount of popular music in the 1960's and the early 1970's in America contained references to drug use and drug experiences, and even some music was recognized symbolically as representative of the feelings and perceptions of drug users, i.e., in its distorted sounds and sound effects.

It also probably is true that drug users often use music to accompany drug experience, particularly when it is hallucinatory, but there is no experimental data known to this author at this time that demonstrates a specific cause-and-effect relationship between music and drugs. In fact, the experience provided by the music itself was recognized by some as a possible alternative to drug use (experimentation, abuse, and even dependency) (Van Stone, 1973).

In the early 1970's, there seemed to be a growing interest in psychic experience, parapsychology, mysticism, some of which has been exploited by writers and therapists in developing various methods for "altered states of consciousness," including the use of music to facilitate such states (Bonny, 1973).

Positive results of drugs in carefully controlled therapeutic settings have been reported in some research where music was introduced, and shown to be of some value in the treatment. One such instance was the use of music as an experience during LSD treatment of alcoholics (Eagle, 1972). The music (recordings) seemed to enhance, enrich, and expand feelings of self-awareness and feelings of relationship with others.

The trend for the use of music therapy with drug treatment programs seems to be similar to its use in other fields, i.e., as a tool in the hands of competent music therapists to support and correlate with other treatment systems, such as reality therapy, or behavioral methods used in re-shaping basic adjustment behaviors of individuals. In addition, music has the advantage of being a fanciful, fantasy-filled medium which has provided diversion and excitement for individuals in all societies for ages, with a potential for being an absorbing, healthful form of "turned-on" activity by people, as an alternate to "turning on" with drugs. At the same time, it must be recognized that music might well be an unhealthy form of over-absorbing activity for some individuals, and a dangerous "cue" for others *for* drug use, or the drug world environment. Clearly, more research is needed in this area to clarify procedures music therapists use, and will use, as drug abuse/dependency continues to cause problems.

LEARNING DISABILITIES

We have been considering problems and treatment of children and adolescents with various diseases, disabilities and disorders ranging from retardation to behavior disorders, including delinquency and drug abuse. Many of these problem children are found not only in special treatment or rehabilitation institutions, but also more and more in special education programs within the schools. Some of these children and adolescents are frequently also in regular classes for another part of the day. This seems to be the trend, i.e., getting away from generalizations about handicapped persons and diagnostic categories, and moving toward recognition of the special problems unique to each individual. In the end, this move is consonant with the ideal of all therapy: *individualization*. A new term has become popular in education to identify this idea: *learning disabilities*. Ideally, each child is considered and evaluated in terms of his *specific learning disabilities*, whether he is considered a member of other special education populations, or categories, or he is from the so-called normal group. Even if he is physically handicapped (deaf, blind, etc.), or mentally retarded, he still should be treated for his specific learning disabilities as much as the otherwise "normal" child who, for example, has reading problems only.

What are some of the specific learning disabilities?

While this term has been applied for several years in education, it has received considerable variation in interpretation. Some writers have approached it from the standpoint of *sources* of learning problems observed in some children in schools who were not easily classified as "retarded" or "physically handicapped." Such sources of problems were visual, hearing, speech, "neurological dysfunctions," and social/emotional deficiencies or problems (Tarnopol, 1971). However, a more comprehensive formulation of theory and definition has been developed by Valett (1969). He related disabilities to the learning abilities normally found or expected in the development of all children, from prenatal stages through infancy, early childhood, preschool and school years.

Valett defines learning disabilities as " ... any specific difficulty in acquiring and using information or skills that are essential to problem solving." He defines a significant disability as one which finds an individual's active performance or achievement in any given ability as being far below his capacity or potential, and further states this as being represented in the school-age child as a discrepancy of one or more years between the child's achievement and his mental age (p. 3).

Specific disabilities may be found in one or more of six major areas of learning: 1) gross motor development; 2) sensory-motor integration; 3) perceptual-motor skills; 4) language development; 5) conceptual skills; and 6) social skills. Under these six major areas Valett lists fifty-three basic learning abilities which he groups in developmental sequence in each area, and operationally defines. Valett recommends identifying and analyzing the problems which may occur in individuals in any of the fifty-three abilities rather than searching out and attempting to treat "underlying causes," viz:

> Primary focus ... must be on the immediate situation and the
> need to take the child forward through careful programming or
> learning tasks appropriate to the child's needs (p. 3).

Possible causes or sources of disabilities, however, are listed as:
1) pre-natal factors; 2) birth trauma; 3) developmental anomalies;
4) emotional deprivation; 5) failure experiences; 6) psychological
frustration; and 7) inadequate instruction. His general description of the characteristics and needs of children with learning
disabilities parallels these causes. Children with repeated failure
experiences, physical and environmental limitations, motivational problems, anxiety, erratic behavior, incomplete evaluation
and inadequate education need special education. These children, according to Valett, "should be given special education
relative to their learning strengths and disabilities instead of educational placement by any gross classification system based primarily on etiological categories (p. 3)."

In other parts of this chapter we have observed examples of
music therapy with children who might have been considered
primarily to have had specific learning disabilities but who were
instead, considered as members of client populations categorized
in other ways, and sometimes placed in institutional clinical
settings on the basis of such categories. The learning disabilities
concept is one which can be used across practically all categories
of children and adolescents who have problems.

In fact, it is quite conceivable that the learning disabilities
concept may even be valuable in considering problems or persons
in every age bracket, no matter what the source of problems may
be. The concept of learning disabilities is often, as with Valett, a
developmental one, i.e., children's problems in school and outside, occur within the developmental, or growth pattern all of us
experience, and as such, problems are often found as part of a
sequence of learning abilities which occur similarly in most persons.

In adults, learning disabilities may be found as a result of an
incompletion of developmental sequences, especially at the levels
of conceptual skills and social skills, or they may occur as a mis-
learned sequence, or as a result of trauma, either physical or

psychological, or both. Language problems and speech disorders are not restricted to children passing through the developmental stages but are found in adults at various age levels, e.g., in persons suffering from stroke, or other brain damaging events.

The application of music therapy in specific learning disabilities has begun to receive attention only in recent years, but some of the techniques have already been described earlier in this chapter, where music therapy with children whose handicaps place them in other client populations or categories, has been discussed. When a therapist is working within a behavioral or learning theory model it is similar to what he would do in work with clients with learning disabilities. This is true also of adult populations, i.e., when problems of clients are viewed as disabilities or distortions of learned behaviors.

CHAPTER 3

MUSIC THERAPY FOR ADULTS

THE same principles of stress, distress, diseases, disorders, and disabilities apply to adults, but there is an even greater variety of problems, a more complex overlap between these categories in the adult human animal. The exact age at which one is considered an adult varies within our own culture, and between cultures. Physically, adulthood is approached from the onset of puberty, but as we have seen in the previous chapter, this marks a period of life called adolescence. From this period to old age (which might be called a period of "obsolescence" in our society) is the largest number of years in man's life span.

Psychological adulthood, or maturity, is a lifelong *continuing* process. We are "growing up" all of our lives. However, general consensus marks adulthood at the point where an individual becomes economically self-sustaining. (Yet we do not "demote" those who are unfortunate enough to be dependent, as on welfare, or like college students, to a sub-adult status! Or do we?)

WHO'S HELPING WHOM?

Adulthood is often divided into youth, middle-age, and old age, but the exact boundaries between each are constantly being redefined, not only as longevity increases, but also as health factors and social factors change. So far as the "Three-D's" (Disease, Disorder, Disability) are concerned, someone has said that the average adult in the USA today has at least one "chronic" disability, disease, or disorder in youth, two in middle-age, and three or more in old age. However this might be, it *is* apparent that those in need of assistance because of poor health (the Three-D's) differ from those *not* needing it only in degree. It should not be depressing, but only realistic then, to recognize that "we are all in the same boat." We are all handicapped or distressed to some extent. It is a matter of persons with less distress helping those with more,

65

not a matter of "we healthy ones" and "they — the unhealthy ones" or "we therapists" and "they — the patients."

This important attitude for every health worker is relatively easier to put into practice by the music therapist, who can promote the feeling of "we are all in the same boat" with a shared music experience. This is a definite advantage in beginning and continuing therapy with adults as well as with children and adolescents who suffer from a variety of disorders.

PROBLEMS AND TREATMENT OF ADULTS WITH BEHAVIOR DISORDERS

Music in therapy with adults has had its most important development and widest acceptance in the realm of behavior disorders. Beginning with World War II and the years immediately following, music therapy became a part of Veterans Administration hospitals, particularly psychiatric, and of the total, or all-over treatment efforts which were being made for military service veterans. This effort influenced new treatment programs in old state "mental" hospitals. All over the USA, music therapy began to be an accepted part of the treatment programs in many hospitals.

Early Institutional Programs

What was a music therapy program like in VA or state hospitals in these early post-World War II years? An example of one program which began following the end of WW II and which is still continuing today in a VA hospital is given below (Michel, 1959; Michel, Gray, 1969).

> The music therapy program at Winter VA Hospital, Topeka, Kansas, had its beginnings in 1946 on an experimental basis as a part of the educational therapy department of the physical medicine and rehabilitation division. During the years 1946-1954 the hospital population varied between 1250 and 1400 patients, and consisted of approximately two-thirds neuropsychiatric and one-third general medical, surgical, and neurological cases. The music therapy program received patients from all of these groups. After about nine months in an

experimental stage, the music therapy program became established officially as a part of the special services division, in accordance with Veterans Administration directives. From this time, more facilities and equipment were provided to carry on music activities for patients, who were assigned or prescribed by physicians on an individual basis as well as in groups. Facilities eventually included an entire one-story ward building which was divided into five practice rooms, two offices, a large group rehearsal room, and other "open" space. Equipment included all of the common musical instruments from pianos and accordians to wind, string, and percussion instruments, plus sheet music, record players, recording machines, and a record library.

As the program developed, numerous musical activities and projects over the hospital became the responsibility of music therapists, ranging from the more diversional or recreational types of activities (ward sings, dances, etc.) to specialized applications, such as background music during surgery, and during insulin coma and electro-shock treatments. Research projects ("pilot studies") were undertaken, in cooperation with medical personnel of the hospital. As the hospital became one of the principal psychiatric training centers for the VA, the presence of many psychiatric residents and other trainees stimulated such studies as well as the general use of music in therapy.

Administrative and medical acceptance of the program was almost *sine qua non*. Over the years there were the changes in personnel, and in program emphasis and organization, but there was always a strong emphasis upon individualized work with patients on a prescription basis.

Procedures for prescribing patients to music therapy included the use of written prescription-forms, filled in by physicians and sent to the music therapy department, with telephone communication between physicians and therapists usually taking place before the patient actually began participation. Participation was on a regularly scheduled basis, mostly at the music clinic (in many cases beginning only after the patient's name had been reached on a waiting list). Progress reports were made by therapists at intervals, as requested by prescribing physicians. Further communication with prescribing physicians was by written replies to progress notes, and by conferences (telephone or personal) between physicians and therapists. At times, music therapists participated in team conferences with physicians and other therapists. During much of this period, the music therapy program was provided with consultative services from the University of Kansas, as well as from the Menninger Foundation.

An important part of the development of the music therapy program at this hospital was its affiliation in 1948 with the University of Kansas for the purpose of providing clinical training to graduate students majoring in "functional music" or music therapy. Clinical training periods were for six months, and student interns (as many as four at a time) provided considerable strength and stimulation to the program. During most of this period, three full-time music therapists were employed in the program.

There were few personnel changes between 1955 and 1967 and general procedures for assignments of patients, periodic reporting on patient progress, and participation of music therapists in "team" meetings remained much the same.

The construction of a new $19 million hospital and the move to it in 1958 tended to emphasize decentralization of treatment for those departments which had enough personnel to place therapists in each hospital unit (of which there are now four).

Music therapy remained a centralized department. There were many advantages to having patients come to a music clinic for appointments, where they could benefit from more specific individual attention of a music therapist. This was true even as the treatment procedures expanded to include the use of nursing assistants responsible for the total planning and execution of programs for specific groups of patients. In such cases, music therapists acted as "consultants" and provided equipment for regular scheduled programs in the adjacent large recreation hall, while at the same time continuing to supervise and instruct individually-assigned patients.

The music therapy program continues in operation today (1975). The hospital population has stabilized at around one thousand patients, and treatment approaches are changing in conformance with general changes in treatment philosophy and theory. It may be said that this program, which was one of the pioneering music therapy programs following World War II, is still considered a vital part of the hospital treatment program, and stands as a model, which has been for over twenty-nine years, a well-accepted, successfully functioning program.

A number of other veterans' hospitals and state hospitals established programs similar to the one at Winter Veterans' Hospital, and developed their own uniqueness and program emphases. Topeka, Kansas, was a good place for music therapy to develop during these early post-WW II years. Not only was there the influence of the Menninger School of Psychiatry, which contracted to train approximately one hundred new psychiatrists every year, but also there was the influence of two other hospitals quite different from the VA (Winter) which were used for this and other psychiatric training programs, i.e., the Menninger Foundation itself — a private hospital, and Topeka State Hospital, a State institution. Within this rich milieu, research was equally emphasized along with training and treatment. This was especially true at first at the Topeka Veterans' Hospital.

Early Research

Research conducted in music therapy at this hospital is exemplified by one study reported at a national music education conference in 1948 (Michel, 1951). The study attempted to determine the effects (especially sedative), of selected recorded background music played through speakers into hospital wards which housed acutely disturbed psychiatric patients. Measurement originally was to be done by comparison of pre- and post-amounts of sedative drugs required by the patients, and by pre-concurrent, and post-observations of individual patient behavior on the ward. The observations were made on forms by ward nursing personnel, the experimenter, and the ward psychiatrist, especially during, before, and just after the times the music was played, i.e., three times during the day: morning at arising time, mid-afternoon, and at bed-time.

Results of the six-week study indicated that mostly positive effects occured. Inadequate controls and the exigencies of a clinical setting prevented accurate observation of the need for and use of sedative drugs by the patients-subjects, but positive effects noted by observers did support the theory that music could influence the general mood of patients, especially at arising and going-to-bed times. Observers noted fewer post-bedtime disturbances by individual patients during the background music period. They also reported an easier arising time with fewer negative or violent patient behaviors. It should be noted that no military bugle calls were used at get-up time; instead, a progressive arrangement of music from quiet, or sedative, to more active, or stimulative, was used, and several patients reported pleasant effects on their mood which persisted throughout the day.

Negative effects were reported for a few individuals and they seemed to be reacting mostly to music which was generally more familiar. Surprisingly, most patients when asked, expressed a preference for the mostly unfamiliar, "classical" type of background music, over the more familiar, popular music.

Summing up this early experiment in using background music, there were strong indications that it was a generally positive factor which should be continued. However, it was noted that careful selection of music was important. The psychiatrist also observed that the selected background music apparently enhanced his interaction with patients while he was on the ward, and that this had not happened when other sound sources such as radios were present.

Recent Institutional Programs

More recent music therapy programs have followed the earlier models in some ways and, at the same time, have been innovative in applying techniques. One example is found in the statement of "Definitions and Goals" of the music therapy program at one southern state hospital:

> ... The significant factor in the use of music as therapy is that the music itself demands a definite structured behavior, one that can be measured through time; at the same time it can be enjoyable (positively reinforcing), motivating, and relaxing. The main goals of music therapy at Southwestern State Hospital follow those of the institution itself: the motivation,

education, and rehabilitation of its residents. The term "education" refers not only to the mentally retarded residents but also those residents with psychiatric disorders who have been deprived of adequate environmental stimulation.[1]

It should be noted that in one sense, "therapy" is always a kind of "education" especially when one defines both as "changed behavior" (see Chapter 1). Another example of music therapy goals and program is that of a northern middle-west private psychiatric hospital, which has adapted to the problems of short-term treatment and a rapid turnover of patients. Behavioral goals are stated along with basic procedures, as follows:[2]

1. Relaxation. Patients are asked to close their eyes for a few minutes, picture themselves in a relaxing place, and really concentrate on that place. This activity is a modification of a systematic desensitization process theory, and is done for two purposes:

   a. To aid concentration. Some people have a very difficult time, concentrating on any one thing for any more than a few moments. The process of having to visualize themselves in a relaxing place helps them to learn to concentrate, the music being a structuring and imagination-stimulating factor, as well as a cue for relaxation.

   b. To learn how it feels to relax, so that an individual may practice the feeling outside therapy sessions, hopefully substituting it for or pairing it up with anxiety producing circumstances.

2. Socialization and verbal interaction. Through an open exchange of ideas during music listening sessions, group members may discuss various attitudes and approaches to the problems of everyday living. Realistic ideas and plans for the future may be tried out in the group and receive

---

[1] Furnished by John B. Walker, RMT, former Director of Music Therapy, Southwestern State Hospital, Thomasville, Ga., 1972.
[2] From intern reports by Gail Hendrick, while interning at Glenwood Hills Hospital, Minneapolis, Minn., Dec., 1971. David Wolfe, RMT, was Director of Music Therapy at that time.

inforcement from group members if viable.

3. Participation in activities. Patients are encouraged to participate in a variety of music activities which may draw them
together as a group where they may gain confidence in group
situations. Many persons have lost, or never acquired the
skills of giving of themselves in social settings, therefore, the
give and take of group participation in music activities may
strengthen such skills.

4. Development of leisure time skills and new interests. Many
persons have increasing amounts of free time which is often
used in brooding over individual problems. Music therapy
may be directed toward introducing these persons to new
skills in music, such as learning how to play guitar, autoharp, and other simpler instruments such as the recorder.
These instruments can be learned in relatively short amounts
of time, at least to a point of enjoyable competence, and can
provide new pathways for more constructive use of leisure
time.

5. Community involvement. Patients are encouraged to participate in activities suited to their interests and which their
home communities have to offer, music-wise. This may give
them something to anticipate upon release from the hospital. Such activities would include choirs, dancing, and
concert-attendance.

The goals are structured to provide patients with possible avenues
through which they may develop a healthier and more positive
approach to the business of everyday living. Goals for music
therapy sessions are discussed with the members of the patient
groups, and purposes for each activity are explained at the beginning or end of the activity.

Community-Based Programs

Within some communities, especially in urban areas, new
treatment facilities are developing, and in several, music therapy
is being provided through community settlement type schools.
Such schools have a long tradition for providing music lessons
and access to the arts by poor people who only pay what they can

afford. Now, music therapy is being provided through such schools, one of which is the Cleveland Music School Settlement. Anita Louise Steele has pioneered music therapy in this school, which offers a variety of services and programs throughout the community to bring music therapy to children and adults with a variety of problems (Steele, 1972).

Community settlement school settings not only are providing a place for music therapy to reach persons needing help but also are beginning to become centers where music and the arts can be a form of preventive therapy for many. Such a center is the Community School of Music and Arts at Mountain View, California, under the direction of Joan Kinnear Van Stone (1975). Like other settlement schools, the Mountain View School offers instruction in the arts, music and dance to many whose economic background would not otherwise make it possible. Lessons are given for fees which can be managed by the pupils, the rest of the costs of the school being made up through contributions. A music therapist is part of the staff and works with clients who are referred by other professionals in the community, i.e., psychiatrists, psychologists, teachers and guidance personnel.

The music therapist also may be assigned to work with those with special needs who are not professionally referred but who are studying with other teachers in the center. In this way there is a continuum bridging the area between those persons with "ordinary" needs and those with special needs, or between education and therapy. This type of center may have great implications for the future as our society changes from its older institutions of active social interaction to newer ones such as the institution of passive television-viewing. There may well be a growing need for community centers which can offer instruction in the arts and music as well as a place for social interaction and for therapy — both curative and preventive.

Community centers serve clients of all ages, and this may be one of the special strengths. There are as yet few places where whole families may come together for recreation, renewal, or treatment as a family. Community arts and music centers also may interact for clients of all ages with other community health agencies and centers, such as those specializing in work with mentally retarded persons, or with those with behavior disorders, or with those whose primary problems are physical disabilities. Some of the relationships may take place by means of the community arts and music center professionals contracting for services and programs to be carried out in other community centers; some of it may take place by way of referral of clients directly to the center. In any case, there seems to be a definite need for more such centers or schools as more and more of the treatment of disordered, disabled, or otherwise distressed individuals takes place within the community, where problems and/or illnesses originate, rather than at traditional hospitals or treatment centers more or less isolated from the community.

For the music therapist there are new challenges to be faced in the community setting. Music activities chosen will need to be even more relevant to the needs and interests of individual clients who receive music therapy.

An example of music relevant to individual patient needs might be instruction on instruments such as guitar, or in dance, where individual skills can be developed, much like music and dance lessons in "normal" society. The difference between music therapy and music instruction is in *how* it is carried out. Music therapists may use music instruction as a structure for helping individuals learn many things besides music, e.g., to improve reading ability, to learn social behaviors needed in certain situations in every day living, or to become oriented to and learn the behaviors of money-handling and shopping problems, while at the same time learning to play the guitar. Another difference is in the therapist, who is working as a member of a community clinical team, contributing his part to a team effort to assist the individual to make a better adaptation *in the place where he lives.*

An example of one program recently inaugurated in a community hospital clinic program lists the following goals of music therapy:[3]

For group activities (Music listening/appreciation; "Pop" choir; Rock group)

---

[3]Provided by Judy Getter, RMT, from the Human Resource Institute division of the Highland Park General Hospital, Miami, Fla., (1974).

aid concentration
Relaxation

— Increase self-esteem and self-confidence
— Increase tolerance of criticism
— Increase social interaction
— Increase responsibility to self and others
— Decrease anxiety and fear of others
— Develop a means of self-expression
and for individual activities (music instruction on guitar, piano, voice, or other instruments)
— Develop consistent work habits and constructive use of leisure time
— Develop skills ... (to combat) ... depression in ones' life
— Develop means of expression of intense feelings
— Increase attention span and concentration, particularly under pressure
— Decrease "giving-up" behavior
— Increase self-esteem through musical accomplishment

Although much of the treatment of persons with behavior disorders is moving out into community centers and settings, there still remains a considerable adult population in older psychiatric institutions, and undoubtedly, music therapists will continue to work in such settings, as well as in the community ones. Some hospitals are making efforts to bridge their work with patients into community centers, and in one instance known to the author, one hospital moved its total program gradually into community facilities. Music therapists at this hospital were able to plan for this transition and to set up programs commensurate with it (Hall, 1969).

Treatment Philosophies

Wherever music therapists do their work they are influenced to some extent by treatment philosophy and/or theory in practice at their locale. Of course, the therapists' own personal philosophy of treatment (and life, as well), plus his training, also determine his procedures, specifically. If, for example, the therapy orientation is psychoanalytic or Freudian based, as it was in the author's early experience, the therapist's general approach would begin as an adjunctive helper to the psychiatrist, who would be considered having primary responsibility for and at least theoretically, the most significant effect upon the patient's treatment. Therefore the music therapist would be expected to depend upon the psychiatrist for goal-setting and for interpretation of the results of therapy. In many such situations however, music therapists do become full-fledged members of the total team (as was the author's experience), and contribute to diagnosis, treatment planning, and evaluation of progress of patients (Michel, 1959, 1960).

One example of one team's work was with a psychotic patient, "E." Weekly team meetings for evaluation and exchange of reports served to keep the team up to date on procedures being followed in treatment. All members of this particular team were considered equal, but of course frequently looked to those with more extensive training for leadership.

The Case of "E."

> E was originally hospitalized for "strange behavior" at the end of his service in the army and just after discharge, in 1946. Once hospitalized he at first appeared more "normal" but soon began to develop some more bizarre behavior, like emitting a loud roar at unpredictable intervals. E was an accomplished pianist and did not object to assignment to music therapy. There he was encouraged to play accompaniments to the therapist's violin playing as a means for developing the "therapeutic relationship," and to give him a creative, expressive outlet for feelings. As treatment progressed, additional aims were set up, such as using the musical experience to encourage reality experiences with others and to discourage fantasizing behavior. This meant placing him in more group activity rather than permitting his listening to recordings alone, or with only one other person.

> Over a period of twelve or fourteen months E improved considerably within the hospital setting, and was given more grounds privileges such as leaving and returning to the ward (which was locked) by himself. He was still unwilling to try to visit relatives away from the hospital, on leave, and also resisted leaving the grounds of the institution even for short periods of time.

When the music therapist left the hospital to take another position, E became quite disturbed, but later settled back into his hospital routine. Meanwhile, the therapist had opportunity to contact the patient's brother, and through communicating what E was like and how he had improved, he influenced the brother to visit E, and ultimately to get him transferred to a hospital nearer the brother, so that frequent visits away from the hospital could be arranged. When last heard from (through the brother), E continued to improve, and to use his musical skills in expressive and relating-to-others ways rather than in withdrawal ways. The brother, also a violinist (like the therapist), had begun to reconstruct his supportive relationship with E through music participation. Hopefully, music therapy had served to assist E in his return to more normal relationships and more comfortable living.

The case of E is derived from actual experiences of the writer during the early 1950's. In the 1970's treatment in music therapy would undoubtedly be different. For one thing, more precise data-taking would occur, with emphasis being placed on specific target behaviors. It is highly probable that the unexpected "roar" from the patient would have been a target behavior, considering the startle effect it had upon the therapist, and everyone nearby. Even after one could at least expect it *might* happen, no one could ever quite prepare for the loud "ROAR"!

Other target behaviors probably would be to discourage "crazy" talk and encourage more realistic conversation, using music contingently, since E did exhibt that music had great reinforcing properties for him. Under such a regime, E's behaviors, which were disordered, excessive, or deficient, might have been more effectively and efficiently changed.

One problem which has always been present in the treatment of persons like E in a hospital setting is how to account for changes and/or improvement in behavior when the patients' life and treatment are so varied within the hospital in terms of different therapies and therapists. How can we tell who or what is most important? Or, in fact, how can we be certain that a patient's communication with family "outside" was not *the* most important factor?

One answer in some of today's hospitals is the development of "token-economy units," where each patient's behavior is made contingent by the use of tokens given for desired behaviors. This may exist for all patients at a rudimentary level of being "charged" tokens for beds and other basic comforts of living. Each patient has an individual chart which carries a record of all his behaviors and of his progress, largely in terms of tokens earned (or lost, i.e., "fined"). Music therapy's contribution more easily may be determined in terms of behaviors of the patient which are influenced through tokens charged or paid for.

Even where a token economy is not in use, modern music therapists may account for their contribution to therapy by carefully recording patients' behaviors during the first music therapy sessions (as a baseline), then selecting and working with target behaviors, and accounting for changes through data observations, e.g., the amount of conversation, or of on-task behavior, or of appropriate social interaction, or of learning specific behaviors such as letter writing. Subsequent follow-up observations of target behaviors in other settings as observed in specific terms, could corroborate any generalization of changes noted in music therapy.

Recent Research

A modern example of accountability as well as of research may be seen in a music therapy project in a state psychiatric hospital, where five women labeled "schizophrenic" were tested by the music therapist for their individual self appraisal, or self-esteem behaviors. They were also observed in behaviors reflecting self-esteem, such as posture, positive verbal statements about themselves, voluntary verbalizations in group settings, and, later, during actual music sessions, their willingness to *try* to learn new music skills as in playing the recorder. The music therapy sessions were structured to try to help the patients learn new skills through which they might increase their self-esteem, especially learning to play a recorder. Post-testing self-esteem inventories as well as on-going behavioral observations substantiated that at least some of these patients exhibited increased self-esteem, attributable to the music therapy (Lim, 1974).

PROBLEMS AND TREATMENT OF ADULTS WHO ARE
DRUG/ALCOHOL ABUSERS AND ADDICTS

Problems

The pairing by slant-mark of "Drug and Alcohol" is not meant to separate these two; indeed, alcohol abuse is recognized as perhaps the most pervasive of all drug abuse. The heading of this section also is not to imply that addiction and abuse in adults is so very different from these problems in younger or older persons.

Sometimes we have been led to believe that drugs, including alcohol, become problems for the young, more often than for other age groups, except perhaps for the usually aging or aged stereotype of the "skid-row bum." Factual studies however, confirm that drug problems are not exclusive to *any* age group.

When do drugs, including alcohol, become problems for people? When is a person labelled an "addict" or an "alcoholic?" When does drug abuse become a problem? Does abuse lead to addiction? Answers to these difficult questions are still being determined by research, but some general statements can be made. Any behavior of abuse, addiction, or even experimentation, becomes a "problem" if it interferes with an individual's personal, social, or work adjustment. This may be determined by the individual but more often is determined by others involved in or near the individual's life, who are affected by the behavior elicited by drug abuse or addiction. For example, the family of an alcoholic may suffer from his/her abnormal behavior while the person is "under the influence" of the drug, or may become economically deprived because of the person's loss of jobs. Other persons, such as victims of robbery by addicts who must steal to support their "habit," are also persons who would label the addiction a problem because they represent "society."

The basic problem may or may not be a physical addiction to drugs. The poor social adjustments of an addicted person may have led him to drug abuse and may actually be primary problems. Most addicts however, have both the problems of addiction (physical need and the threat of painful withdrawal symptoms if

they stop using the drug), and the problems of adjustment underlying, and resulting from the drug abuse.

Treatment

No universal methods of cure have yet been found, short of
complete control of one person's life by others. A number of
treatment approaches have enjoyed moderate if not total success,
such as Alcoholics Anonymous (AA), and the Daytop and Synanon types of programs for persons addicted to drugs. All of these
programs involve group interaction and peer influence as well as
requirement of commitment from the individual who joins.

Some psychiatric approaches have involved various forms of
psychotherapy, as well as chemotherapy, or the use of other drugs
to counteract or help control the addictive drug. One drug, *antabuse,* if taken regularly, produces a strong aversion in the person
against imbibing of alcohol. If imbibed, the person becomes
nauseously ill. However, continuation of treatment by use of
antabuse ultimately depends upon the individual. LSD (lysergic
acid diethylamide) has been used experimentally with some alcoholics and other drug abusers to produce emotionally "deep" and
"mind-expanding" experiences in individuals as an intended
means of producing "insight" and a type of conversion toward
changed behavior by the person.

The Daytop and Synanon type groups utilize a close, daily,
living-together group, with frequent meetings and discussions
which stress total honesty and realism on the part of all participants toward themselves and toward the groups. In such a de-
manding environment many individuals have managed to learn
new patterns of behavior and to become free of drug addiction.

Music has been used mostly in a casual way with several of the
above approaches to treatment. So far, little research has been
done but there appears to be an important role for music therapeutically as a facilitator of group interaction, a facilitator of
mood-setting for emotional, insightful experiences, and a possible new leisure time activity of sufficient strength of interest
and involvement to substitute for drug abuse, especially that from
which an individual may be seeking "turn-on" or "peak"

experience (see Discussion in Ch. 2).

A recent research attempted to determine the facilitative effect of music for relaxation exercises, designed to help alcoholics learn how to combat anxiety and tension which may lead to excessive drinking (Stephens, 1974). Teaching relaxation techniques, especially attempting to help individuals pair such techniques with feelings of tension and anxiety, has been done in some hospitals recently, along with efforts to get individuals to make personal commitments to treatment through contracting agreements. Music has shown its potential value as a cue in assisting individuals to remember *how* to relax under conditions producing distress, i.e., consciously recalling tunes associated with relaxation seems to help individuals resist distress and tension through relaxation procedures.

Future research and clinical experience may further define the role of music within treatment systems now being used for adults who have problems with drug abuse/addiction. In addition, music in itself may prove to be an effective counteractant if it can be directed toward strengthening an individual's self-esteem, or providing an outlet for tension, not only as a cue for relaxation but also as a release-type activity, which may substitute for the "release" found through drugs.

PROBLEMS AND TREATMENT OF ADULTS
WHO ARE "RETARDED"

"Retarded" adults are found not only as grown-up, institutionalized children, but also as neglected persons in our society, often within economically and socially deprived populations. Parents and relatives of retarded children have been instrumental through local and national organizations or associations for retarded children, in calling attention to this neglect and influencing action to allow retarded children opportunities to develop their individual potentialities. These associations in the early 1970's became Associations for Retarded *Citizens,* thereby recognizing that there are adults who are retarded, and that they can be helped and do have the right, *as citizens,* to expect help. Legal rights of these persons, both within and outside of institutions were carefully scrutinized and revised during these years.

Specifically, problems of retarded adults parallel those of retarded children, except that *more* responsible behavior is usually
expected of adults. Until the 1970's, many adult retardates remained in institutions largely because they had not been taught
responsible social behaviors, nor work skills to enable their integration into society. It was gradually realized and recognized that
many adult retardates could be *habilitated,* or taught basic, essential living skills to enable them to assume more independence and
responsibility. Vocational workshops in institutions, and sheltered workshops in the community, along with "half-way
houses" to provide life skills training facilities within the community, began to enable many persons to grow toward better
adaptation in our society.

Music Therapy

In much the same way that music is being used in therapy and
special training and education for retarded children, it is being
applied with adults. Specifically, music therapists, like other
therapists and teachers, provide learning experiences to meet the
individual needs of retarded adults. This may be in terms of learning basic self-help skills used in daily living, which would enable
a person to move out of the institution into a community facility
where he may receive some supervision and guidance as he makes
his adjustments in daily living. In one hospital, music therapists
taught individuals such skills as teeth-brushing, bed-making,
and personal grooming, using special songs composed to teach
these things in a timed sequence. Music in the form of group
participation in listening and dancing activities was used as a
reinforcer for those patients achieving the desired behaviors.
Points or chips entitling the patients to participate were earned by
their progress in learning, or trying to learn the desired behaviors.

In community settings such as sheltered workshops and half-
way houses, retarded adults are stimulated and assisted in learning not only the desired self-care skills, but they are also taught
basic work skills to enable them to begin to assume certain types
of jobs. Simple, but coordinated movement necessary in some

jobs, such as assembling parts, have been taught these persons through music, such as rhythm or percussion instrument playing (for improving coordination), and songs which guide the person through the sequence of behaviors in a work task. Again, reward value of music, such as learning to play more sophisticated instruments like guitar, has been found to be effective in reinforcing learning for work skills, and even, in some cases, for motivating individuals to accept and work through vocational rehabilitation work evaluation tests. Research undoubtedly will enable further applications in such community settings for the use of music in teaching and reinforcing the learning of basic skills, both social and economic.

One of the most important aspects of adaptation is the constructive use of leisure time. Music obviously has value since it has been used by man for many ages not only in many functional ways, but also as a form of play, and a *constructive* structuring of time. For retarded adults, this may be one of the most important aspects of habilitation which can enable individuals to become more independent in living away from institutional settings. In addition, music may well serve such individuals as it serves all persons who make use of it, as a means of communication, expression, and outlet for feelings. Persons who are "retarded" are *not* retarded in respect to feelings; they have as many needs for expression of feelings as anyone, and music can serve them as well as it can all of us.

PROBLEMS AND TREATMENT OF ADULTS WHO ARE PHYSICALLY HANDICAPPED

Problems of adults who are physically handicapped include many of those already noted with children and adolescents, i.e., locomotion and coordination, visual disabilities, hearing disabilities, and speech problems. Causes of the variety of problems arising from these broad categories may be similar to those for children and adolescents such as diseases, or accidents, or congenital, but they also may be more complex in origin and may even *derive from* psychological (behavior disorder) problems as well as become associated with *secondary* psychological problems.

Again, it should be noted that an individual's specific problems of adaptation and adjustment resulting from physical disabilities are often similar to those found in children and adolescents, as well as the kinds of problems found across many other diseases, disorders, and disabilities. Because of this similarity of problems, therapists, including music therapists, can adapt their methods across patient populations in somewhat similar ways, always taking into account, of course, that individuals are unique and different and may need specific approaches in each instance.

One area of physical disability not specifically considered for children and adolescents, and which is present in that age group as well as in all age groups, is that caused by or consisting of physical disorders which are more or less chronic. Such problems as allergies, arthritis, certain chronic infections (such as ear), as well as chronic diseases such as *myaesthenia gravis* (muscular) and *muscular dystrophy,* affect millions of persons, inflict suffering, and cause multiple handicaps in the psychological and social adjustment areas. What does music therapy have to offer these persons? Again, the specific problems are similar to those encountered with other patient populations, i.e., individual problems of anxiety, tension, social relationships, and of loss of self-esteem, of motivation, or of ability to concentrate.

Music may be structured as an *encourager* as well as a memory cue or *facilitator,* toward specific goals in treatment of such individuals. This applies as well to persons suffering from the more conventional physical disorders mentioned previously.

Not only do adults suffer physical disabilities from accidents, such as auto, which happen to them as they interact with their external environments, but they also suffer from internal "accidents" which may result from a variety of causes. One such common accident is stroke, sometimes called cerebral vascular accident (CVA). General communicative disorders such as aphasia may ensue from these internal accidents, as well as from external ones.

Music therapists are today encountering adults with physical disabilities in a variety of clinical settings. Easter Seal and United Cerebral Palsy clinics have been mentioned earlier. Other places might include rehabilitation centers, such as a regional one at Florida State University, physical therapy clinics which are part of hospitals, and extended care centers, where persons requiring continued care may be treated.

A music therapist may be asked to assist with speech problems by a speech pathologist, or with coordination exercises by the physical therapist. The RMT also finds his unique place not just in providing the special structuring and reinforcing properties of his medium in working with clients; he also may provide group music activity which can become facilitative for re-socialization with persons who must learn to adapt to new physical limitations, and to *accept* themselves, as well as *express* themselves with others. Music therapists are being recognized for such contributions and are regular members of treatment teams in many settings.

PROBLEMS AND TREATMENT OF ADULTS WHO ARE LAW-BREAKERS

It is still a problem within our society to determine whether law-breakers should be treated or should be punished. But by and large, more treatment — at least rehabilitation (treatment over a longer period of time) — is accepted as a need.

Treatment — or rehabilitation — may well include music therapy for adult law-breakers, and in much the same way as it was described previously for juvenile delinquents. Whether or not a law-breaker who is incarcerated is ever "cured," he can be given the chance, and encouraged to learn new behaviors which may enable him to make a better adaptation when he returns to society (or even within the prison, if he is a long-termer).

The learning of music itself may have important therapeutic value. The writer knows of one instance where a group of young men organized a popular music "combo" while in prison, and when they were released continued to play as a commercial group, and supplemented their living by doing so. This was an instance of unorganized, informal music therapy, since no trained therapist with a goal-directed program was involved, but it seems a worthy example of how music therapy perhaps *should* work in some cases!

Within some correctional institutions, inmates who have had diagnosed personal learning and/or social deficits may be helped through music therapy. Using music in its structuring, facilitating, and reinforcing ways, music therapists may assist inmates to learn new skills, and new behaviors which may make it easier for them to adapt to society when they return. It is well know that prisons may become "training schools" for better criminal techniques and additional contacts with the criminal society upon release from prison for many inmates. It also is known that many persons who are released from prison fail to readjust not only because of prevailing attitudes of the public toward "ex-cons" and the effects of the informal "training schools" within the walls but also because they lack adequate leisure skills. Once back in a community, these persons need all the help and supervision they can get if they are to become contributing members of society, but ability to use leisure time constructively is of vital importance.

As yet, few examples exist of music therapy applications in penal settings. The *potential* applications and need for more research in such settings seem obvious, and it is a great challenge to music therapy as a field. Music therapy definitely has a place in penal settings when the training schools are organized by the authorities rather than by the inmates, toward rehabilitative goals rather than refined criminal techniques.

PROBLEMS AND TREATMENT OF ADULTS WHO "HAVE BECOME TOO OLD"

Problems and Point of View

The study of the process and problems of aging is called *"gerontology;"* the treatment of persons with problems associated with ageing is called *"geriatrics."* The term "geriatric" is sometimes used as a somewhat derogatory substitute for "older person," with or without problems. In this sense it may reflect a fairly general attitude toward older people in western society: one of decreased value, of "obsolescence," which is held mostly by those also *believed* by many who are older. This prevailing attitude affects much of what is developing in the field, such as improved medical and behavioral techniques of treatment. Such improvements mean less when the general attitude about the worth of older people is negative or even if it is non-caring, or ignoring. Possibly the main problems of older adults then, are with societal attitudes, and perhaps these should be the focus of effort by therapists and older persons who are concerned.

One of the best ways of expressing concern is through a direct involvement with the "geriatric" population. Improvements in their health and the contributions of elderly people to society may be the best material for teaching other members of society about the continuing and increasing value of older persons. Thus, the music therapists might conceivably influence public opinion, if he were able to develop a form of musical "commercial" for and by older people, e.g., by helping them to demonstrate their humanity and their contributions through music and music performance.

What are some of the facts about the geriatric population today? One columnist has summarized important points as follows:

—Elderly people (sixty-five & over) constitute 10.3% of our population in the USA, and this will soon be 15 %.
—Less then 3% of National Institute of Mental Health funds are spent on geriatric problems.
—No university or medical school yet has established a special chair of geriatric medicine.
—People over sixty-five account for more suicides than any other age group.
—Nursing home populations are 80% female, and more women sixty-five or over, than men are in mental hospitals (Alexander, 1974).

This particular writer coupled the presentation of these facts with a reference to the advances in medicine, such as mechanical replacements for vital organs, which lend themselves to the increase of numbers of older persons in our society. She raised the question of our neglect in deciding what to do with this increasing part of our population, and the many unsolved problems due to neglect in studying further the causes of ill health in older people. The former problem is probably the most important one because it reflects the value system of our society, our general acceptance of the idea that people decrease in value at older ages and become obsolescent.

Part of this problem of value may lie in some of the myths about ageing. One writer has listed ten such myths (Snider, 1974):

1. Man cannot add significantly to his life span.
2. Greater health longevity can be achieved but not in the near future.
3. Delaying old age will impose greater economic burdens on society.
4. Extended life spans will pose difficult new social problems, particularly between the older and younger generations.
5. Extended life span will add to the population explosion.
6. We ought not to tinker with aging because the way it is now is the way nature wanted it.
7. Death of the elderly makes way for new, perhaps better, forms of evolved life (obsolescence idea).
8. Increasing the life span of the human species will result in our being surrounded by more people who are decrepit, unsightly, and dependent.
9. The progress being made now is about all that can be expected.
10. Man has the potential to become physically immortal.

All of these myths are myths because they have no basis in fact. Probably the most dangerous ones blocking progress are numbers 3, 4, 5, 7, and 8, because they reflect attitudes toward ageing and the elderly in many parts of our society. If people in good health between the ages of 65-85 years could remain employed (#3) they could make more positive contributions to society (at least as consumers). Physically healthy older people can have a longer period for self-development (#4), and can learn new ways of adapting and relating to others of all ages. Extending the life span by twenty years would add 28% to the total population over a forty-year period (#5), then level off. This is not significant when compared to increasing or high birth rates, in the population explosion problem. (While this is a decreasing problem in the USA, birth rates remain high around the world.)

No studies have yet shown better forms of life are developed by succeeding generations overtaking present ones (#7) or by the passing on of older forms. And, the slowing down of the aging process would push the fraction of the population of elderly in despair and disrepair up to higher age levels, rather then increasing life span, but decrease the fraction of those who are disabled (#8).

Treatment

If we can dispel some of these myths and work for a more positive attitude about the value of older persons in our society many of the "problems" in geriatrics will begin to be solved. Meanwhile, there still remain many problems which are special to the elderly. What can the music therapist do? The many varied possibilities for participation in music are as available to the elderly as to other age groups. As a stimulant for movement, music can generally encourage and regulate physical exercise with all of its attendant possible positive benefits (coordination, mobility, circulatory-respiratory improvement, etc.). Likewise, such stimulation can increase mental alterness and lead to more awareness of the present, and of the individual self, toward restoration of self-care and positive involvement and independence.

Music Therapy

Specifically, music therapy may be applied to groups with similar needs and to individuals with special problems. Using pre-, concurrent-, and post-measures of psycho-physical functions such as motor coordination, and of self-esteem, music therapists may plan and program specific activities for individuals, both in one-to-one and in group situations.

One woman resident of a nursing home was despondent, inattentive, and generally inactive, primarily because of limited functioning of her right arm and hand as the result of a stroke. A music therapist helped her rediscover her interest in music, and, working closely with the physical therapist, she devised exercises which the client could do in rhythm to music. The number of times the woman could squeeze a soft rubber ball to music gradually increased over a short period of time, and she could notice her own progress, as it was marked on a chart. Soon she was able to use the hand and arm well enough to begin studying and playing a small organ. Her progress in playing the organ led her to increased interaction with other residents, as she was encouraged by the therapist to share her music with others. Ultimately, she developed her skills sufficiently to want to display her new interest to her children and grandchildren, and she began to go home more frequently on visits. The long range goal of therapy was that she would be sufficiently confident and healthy to live more independently, perhaps in a "board and care" home, from whence she might travel to a day care center, continuing to study music, and rediscovering a useful life for herself (Ross, 1973).

SUMMARY

Music therapy for adults encompasses an ever-widening scope of applications. Primarily used for persons with behavior disorders (diagnosed as mentally ill or emotionally disturbed), it now is finding increased application with persons suffering from many other types of disorder, disease, or disability.

Adulthood is roughly divided into youth, middle age, and old age stages. Music therapy is used successfully for many persons in each of these categories, as a form of constructive, facilitative activity and as reinforcement of learning new adaptive skills and behaviors.

A program in existence since 1946 at the Topeka Veterans Administration Hospital (Kansas), was described as an example of a model music therapy program in a psychiatric hospital. One of the early experimental research projects explored the effects of background music upon psychiatric patients who were considered severely disturbed, and found many positive results in terms of promotion of a more restful atmosphere at bedtime, a more cheerful atmosphere at arising time in the morning, and a more positive and communicative attitude on the part of patients toward the ward psychiatrist when he made his daily visits on the ward. It also discovered possibly harmful effects of such background music when some instances of music familiar to certain individuals seemed to reinforce undesirable, unhealthy thinking and behavior. Few studies of this sort have been done in the intervening years, but it would appear to be a needed area for research.

More recent programs in hospitals were described, along with therapy goals set forth for such programs. In addition, community health facilities were described, with the applications and potential applications for music therapy being pointed out. One recent experience in the community mental health setting, a psychiatric ward in a general hospital, was not mentioned but is added here: effects of music activities and background music seemed to have a place for patients who are admitted to such facilities as acutely disturbed persons, in terms of furnishing 1) reassurance, 2) distraction from the disturbing episodes which caused hospitalization, 3) promotion of feelings of security and relaxation, and 4) a general tension-reducing effect which could be seen to be reflected in needs and requests for medical sedation at night by many of the patients. In addition, the possibility of establishing contact with patients at this acute stage for later continuation of treatment at other community facilities was an important finding.

Community music school settlements were mentioned as one way of developing the possibility of follow-up work with disturbed adults in communities, as well as the type of center which can serve communities in many ways, including as a kind of preventive medicine for many persons. Centers in Cleveland and in California were mentioned as examples of such centers, which serve not only adults, but all ages.

Since many persons continue to be treated in psychiatric hospitals on a long-term basis, a case example of music therapy with one such patient was presented, as an illustration of the form of treatment in the past and the development of more precision and accountability in methods used today.

Music therapy for adults who are alcohol and drug abusers or addicts was described in terms of recent findings, which make use of music as an aid to learning how to reduce anxiety and tension, as well as a possible alternate "turn-on" or addictive activity which has few if any of the bad side effects of drugs.

For those adults who are retarded and need special care inside institutions or in the community, music therapy has much to offer, not only as constructive leisure time activity but also as a useful facilitator of learning, i.e., learning of basic social and vocational skills.

Finally, music therapy with older persons, "geriatrics," was reviewed as a useful, constructive, and rehabilitative therapy as well as a possible vehicle for influencing a change in attitude on the part of the general public in this country toward older persons. This attitude, one of "obsolescence" toward aging people, needs to be changed if older citizens are to enjoy their later years and continue to make the contribution to society as a whole, of which they are capable.

CHAPTER 4

THE PROFESSIONAL MUSIC THERAPIST RESPONSIBILITIES AND ATTITUDES

Since the founding of the National Association for Music Therapy (NAMT) in 1950, much has been said and written about the responsibilities of the professional music therapist. Probably the most important thing which seems to resound consistently is that the music therapist *is* a professional person, and should consider himself in that light. What is a professional? This word has many meanings today: professional athlete, professional politician, professional soldier, etc. In this general sense it means one who is dedicated to a certain pursuit as a lifetime career. Originally, "the professions" consisted of the law, medicine, theology, and teaching. Today however, a dictionary definition states that a profession is "a calling requiring specialized knowledge and often long and intensive academic preparation." (Webster, 1963).

Webster's definition only gives the nature of a profession — that it is a calling and often requires long academic preparation. It does not define responsibilities or attitudes of a profession in general, nor for any special professions. Who or what is the "model" for the profession of music therapy? First, in terms of length of preparation, which basically is at the bachelor's degree level, the model most likely is the teacher, whose basic preparation is the four-year college course. Over the past fifty years, however, certain helping people in the health field also have developed basic academic preparation at the bachelor's degree level, and music therapists, as relatively late arrivals on the scene, may well take these persons as models. Occupational therapists, physical therapists, and nurses (the registered nurse may or may not take the four-year academic degree program to become registered) have

been in the health field for some time. Their training differs from
teachers in that some form of clinical training or apprenticeship
is a requisite of the degree (although practice teaching required
for teacher preparation is sometimes called "internship") and it
often comes *after* the academic work is completed. So the music
therapist may model himself professionally after several types of
health workers.

At the apex of health workers are those trained through the
doctoral level. Doctors of medicine as well as doctors of philosophy provide the ultimate "model" of professional responsibility
and attitudes. The "M.D.", of course, is most often found in the
most responsible health service positions, but increasingly, the
Ph.D. in psychology, sociology, or other related fields, may be
found in positions at a similar level.

How do these "models" influence the ideal sense of responsibility of the professional music therapist? If asked, most of the models would probably respond that they try to follow a certain code
of ethics, commonly called "professional ethics." One such code
of behavior perhaps was first expressed in the ancient "Hippoc-
ratic oath" of physicians. Essentially, this is a pledge of concern
for every human life, and the pledge to care for those in distress
from whatever cause.

"Professional ethics" then means a basic pledge of concern for
assisting distressed human beings. The term also implies a code of
behavior in dealing with patients, i.e., a basic respect of the individual's right of privacy, and his right to be treated with dignity
— as an *individual* and unique human being. In practice, this
means protecting the rights of individuals when they are in one's
care. An example would be the extreme carefulness exercised by
all health professionals in keeping diagnostic and treatment information about an individual patient strictly confidential, that
is, protecting it from dissemination to persons other than those
directly connected with treatment of the individual.

Responsibilities, then, may be modeled somewhat from other
professional health workers and their codes of ethics. The music
therapist's professional responsibility means knowing the ethics
of health workers in general and subscribing to these general
concepts, especially toward patients. To this might be added the

responsibility of every college graduate to *continue* his own education. In music therapy, this would mean an active effort to keep abreast of the latest developments in the field, and to apply them in his own practice when feasible. In part this is done by maintaining membership and an active interest in his own professional organization (such as the NAMT).

Where do attitudes come in? We have been discussing attitudes in general as we describe the *basic* professional responsibilities of the field. It seems obvious that a primary attitude would be one of willingness, or even of eagerness, to learn and accept the responsibilities of one's profession. Beyond this probably the next most important attitude for the professional music therapist to seek to develop is part of the responsibility for continuing one's own learning and developing the "scientific attitude." This is a nebulous but real ideal which should be cultivated from a base of "open-mindedness" about the world and about oneself, as well as toward learning the "know-how" concerning research methods and techniques. Essentially, it means a willingness to accept the temporary nature or status of *all* knowledge, and the high probability for change over a period of time in any area of "certainty" about "facts." When new evidence is presented, one must be willing not only to question and test it rigorously, he must also be prepared to accept change and to change his own concepts.

Finally, attitudes form a kind of "bent," an inclination to react in a certain, predictable way when certain stimuli are presented. Attitudes too, may change, but some may be rooted in belief, and more difficult to change than others. It is the author's contention that it is desirable to seek to develop such "belief" attitudes, when it concerns professional responsibilities, ethics, and dedication to one's "calling."

It is important for one to have certain substantial footings in beliefs or concepts before he can even challenge them; therefore, it is important for the music therapist to have a base of belief in his own profession. Perhaps this might be supplied for some by a "Music Therapist's Creed" suggested by the author in an earlier article (Michel, 1962):

> I believe in music therapy because I believe in *music* as an effective, communicative, therapeutic tool, and as an important

and necessary part of every man's life. I believe in music therapy because I believe in *therapy* — that is, I believe that sick people can and should be helped. I believe in music therapy because I believe that the "essence of life" is in what *contributions* I can make to it, and that my chosen profession provides me with a unique and wonderful means for making such contributions.

WHO ARE WE?

Relative to other therapists and health professionals, *who are music therapists?*

In special education there are teachers of the deaf, teachers of the blind, teachers of the retarded, and teachers of the educationally handicapped and emotionally handicapped children. There are also learning disabilities specialists, and other special teachers for handicapped children. Most of these teachers employ special teaching methods in order to provide handicapped children access to the same general education available to everyone in our society.

Other special teachers and therapists include speech pathologists, who work with children and adults exhibiting one or more symptoms of disordered communication (speech and language). Speech pathologists make use of special methods and techniques in working with the many different kinds of clients who exhibit speech and language problems. Communicative disorder is the primary symptom, but it is also obvious that speech pathologists must be concerning themselves with working with the whole person.

Audiologists and deaf education specialists focus on assessment of hearing problems and adaptation to them, again, like other specialists, using special methods and techniques both in diagnosis and in treatment, or special education.

Recreation therapists use the process of activities and games and other leisure time pursuits (sometimes including recreational music) as their medium for working with clients of all types of disorder, disease, or disability, and in this way, are similar to music therapists. Occupational therapists likewise use activities, especially those associated with arts and crafts, coupled with their knowledge of physical and psychological needs of many differently diagnosed clients, to treat them.

In some treatment programs such as those found in the Veterans Administration hospitals, other special therapists are found, such as those called "educational therapists," "industrial therapists," and "vocational rehabilitation therapists and counselors." These special therapists use special methods and techniques akin to their own specialty, to treat their clients. And, often several of these specialists work together cooperatively in "treatment teams."

As noted in the first chapter, music therapy first developed in many places after World War II as one of the activity therapies and in this context, as an activity medium, music therapy is similar to other activity therapies. What then differentiates music therapists from other specialists? It is almost too obvious to state that the medium of music therapists i.e., music, is what makes music therapy unique, but like many truisms, the simple, obvious answer also remains true.

Compared with other special therapists and teachers, music therapists do have the most unique medium with which to work. It is appropriate for us to say that as music therapists we are *generalists* with a *special* medium. We work with all types of clients of all ages, using music as our tool. Other activity therapists do not have the kind of special medium that music therapists have, although some, like recreation and occupational therapists, do make use of a variety of media. We, as music therapists, and as generalists are more like the other activity therapists than we are like special education teachers who usually are more specialized with respect to client populations with whom they are trained to work. Among all of the special teachers and therapists perhaps music therapists are more like speech pathologists (speech and language therapists) than any other therapists. We deal with all populations and often are most concerned with what can be designated as communicative disorders. Yet, we are still unique, by virtue of the fact that we are trained to use our unique medium of music.

Looking at this special medium — music — we find that many persons seem to misunderstand and to view it only in the terms of either professional music performance, music education, or music appreciation, and thereby underestimate its great versatility and wide application to persons regardless of background or training in music. Music in our society today is pervasive, pleasurable, and sometimes even undesirable and inescapable. But it is seldom, if ever, possible to ignore. Good or bad, wanted or unwanted, it is a powerful influence in our every day lives, and in the hands of a skilled music therapist, it is a powerful therapeutic tool.

DEVELOPMENTS IN OTHER COUNTRIES

Music therapy — "An idea whose time has arrived?" In the 1960's and 1970's this phrase did seem applicable to many parts of the world where music therapy was gradually becoming used more extensively and the term "music therapy" was not so strange to so many people.

We have already noted the beginning of music therapy as a widespread practice in the USA beginning in the post WW II years, and also have noted that the *idea* of music therapy is as old as the history of mankind itself. Earlier examples of clinical applications of music in therapy in this century may be found but the widespread use which was stimulated by the need for treating war veterans no doubt caused the greatest stimulus for the establishment of music therapy as a profession.

In other countries it is interesting perhaps to observe that treatment of war veterans had a greater priority for those who were victorious in the war (e.g., the Allies after WW-II) than in those who were defeated. Outside the USA, probably the most widespread use of music in therapy developed in England, where the British Society for Music Therapy marks its beginnings in the late 1950's. On the other hand, music therapy as an organized effort was only being reported in Japan in the late 1960's. This is relatively true also of the efforts in West Germany and other European countries which were associated with the Axis powers. Some of the countries which were defeated by Axis powers, (Germany, Italy and Japan) such as France, Holland, and the Scandinavian countries have also reported music therapy developments only in these recent years. In another part of the world, Australia also has had reports of music therapy developments in the 1960's, but only isolated and rare reports of interest or work in the field have been received from other continents: Africa, Asia, or even South America.

However, there were new developments which were reported in the late 1960's, and early 1970's, e.g., there was a new, strong movement developing in Columbia in 1974 formed by a group of medical doctors and called the Sociedad Antiqueña-De Musicoterapia. This group began at the University of Antiquena in Medellin and published its first journal, "Revista," in December of 1974 (Director of the association is Dr. L. Alberto Correa C., and the secretary is Dr. Alfredo Rolando Ortiz).

In Brazil there was an enthusiastic group who formed a national association and held the first national conference on music therapy at Porto Alegre, through the University of Rio Grande of the South (a federal university) in 1970. The group was headed by Doctora Di Pancaro who had established a music therapy department at the University, and the conference included participants not only from other parts of Brazil but also from other South American countries such as Argentina, Peru, Venezuela, and Columbia. In Argentina another strong movement already was taking place under the leadership of Dr. Benenzon of Buenos Aires. Juliette Alvin, Chairman of the British Society for Music Therapy, had given lectures to the Argentinian group in the late 1960's (the author had the privilege of representing the NAMT at the first Brazilian conference in 1970, at the invitation of the Brazilian association. He also gave a week of lectures in Porto Alegre).

In North America, besides in the United States, interest in music therapy was developing strongly in Canada, which saw its own Canadian Association of Music Therapy established in 1974. Interest in music therapy was evidenced in Mexico and some Central American countries, but no organized movements had developed by the mid-1970's.

On the other side of the Atlantic, the oldest and strongest movement in music therapy is seen in England, where it has developed largely under the leadership of Juliette Alvin. The British Society for Music Therapy was formed in 1958, and was first called the

"Society for Music Therapy and Remedial Music" (it was changed to its present name in 1967). The Society now organizes annual conferences and publishes a journal three times a year *(British Journal of Music Therapy)*. It is now associated with the Guildhall School of Music and Drama in London, where a one-year, post-graduate course is offered which leads to the diploma (LGSM) in Music Therapy. Juliette Alvin continues to be one of the important leaders (as Chairman of the British Society) in the 1970's, and is internationally known through her lecturing in the USA, in South America, and in Japan, and through her books and articles (Alvin, 1966, 1968, 1969). (Miss Alvin made it possible for the author to become acquainted with many programs and therapists in Great Britain while he was there, September 1970 - March 1971.)

Other therapists of note in England are Frank Knight, RMT, who has worked as a music therapist in Canada and the USA, and who, in 1970-71, referred to himself as an "Ancient Briton," and in 1975 was still working in several positions as a part-time music therapist, principally in the Croydon area of Surrey county. He has contributed articles to several journals and magazines, and remains a vital and positive force for music therapy, not only in England, but in Europe through international meetings, and in other parts of the world.

Another related effort in England is the program at Dartington College of the Arts, at Totnes, Devon. Special materials and approaches for music with exceptional children have been developed through a project sponsored by the Carnegie Foundation, and these are channeled to music and classroom teachers by means of conferences and a book, *The Slow Learner and Music* (Dobbs, 1970). While this is not music therapy *per se*, it is related in the sense of having developed musical materials appropriate for use by music therapists as well as music teachers and classroom teachers. (The author was privileged to have visited with Mr. Dobbs and others at the Totnes school in 1971.)

In 1974 Clive Muncaster, RMT, returned to England from music therapy training in the USA to establish a program in music therapy at the Borocourt Hospital for the retarded, near Reading. Muncaster established the first overseas internship program approved by the NAMT, at the Borocourt hospital. (It was affiliated with The Florida State University, Tallahassee, from which the first two interns at Borocourt were assigned, in 1974.)

DEVELOPMENTS IN EUROPE. Music therapy has developed in an organized way in several European countries, especially during the 1960's and 1970's, but there is not any sort of "European Music Therapy" as such, according to DeBeir (1974). Instead, individual countries have formed associations and have developed programs, many of which have been influenced by American music therapists and by other theorists and therapists in Europe and England.

In the Netherlands, a Dutch Foundation for Music Therapy (Stichting voor Muziektherapie) was established in 1969, and in cooperation with the Dutch Association for Expressive and Creative Therapy, publishes a quarterly journal, *Documentatiebladen*. The foundation had established special lectures and the beginning of training courses by 1970 and had invited foreign music therapists as lecturers on a regular basis. (The author was privileged to be one of these lecturers in March, 1971.) Dutch music therapists earlier had received international attention, especially Van Uden, in their work with the deaf, using music therapy techniques. Lievegoed earlier (1939) had published his book on *Measure, Rhythm, Melody: Foundations for a Therapeutic Use of Musical Elements,* and Holthaus later published his treatise, *Music Therapy,* which dealt with his rhythm tests as the basis for therapy through music (1970).

In Scandinavia, a foundation was established for furthering the training of music therapists ("Nordesk Forbund vor Pedagogesk Musik-therapie"). It was to serve as a parent organization for groups in Norway, Denmark, Sweden, and Finland. Denmark developed its own association and began to organize workshops and seminars to train music therapists. By 1970, a group in Oslo, Norway had begun to develop a Norwegian association and had sponsored foreign lecturers and courses. (The author was privileged to be one of the lecturers in Oslo in March, 1971.) By 1973, one of Norway's leading music therapists, Even Ruud, had returned to Oslo to further the development of music therapy in Norway, following his study in the USA (certificate in therapy, and M.M. in therapy, F.S.U., 1973).

In West Germany, Berlin is the center for three organizations promoting music therapy, the most effective one of which according to DeBeir, is the German Committee on Music Therapy (Deutscher Ausschuss fur Musiktherapie), which was founded at the first German congress on music therapy in 1971 (DeBeir, 1974). Hans Willms provided the first report of this meeting, and also founded a separate group, the Berlin Workshop on Music Therapy. A third organization was formed by Maria Schuppel (Musiktherapeutische Arbeitsstatte). In Berlin, there is one private educational facility to train music therapists, an Institute for Music Therapy, headed by Johanna von Schulz, and an internship under Willms' direction was established in 1973 (DeBeir).

As early as 1958 H. R. Teirich, a psychiatrist in Freiburg, had published a book which translated several articles by foreign music therapists into German (Teirich, 1958). Later, Josef published a book on the use of music as a part of the education of the mentally handicapped (Josef, 1970). Wolfgart published a book on the use of Orff Schulwerk techniques in the education and therapy of handicapped children (Wolfgart, 1971). In recent years, many American music therapists have "discovered" Orff Schulwerk as a technique which they employ in their practices.

In East Germany, a Division of Music Therapy as a part of a medical association for psychiatry, was organized in 1969, with Christa Kohler and Christoph Schwabe as founders. This organization promotes workshops and symposia on music therapy which are held at intervals through the year. So far, the group has no official journal, but Schwabe has published a book, *Music-Therapy With Neuroses and Functional Disturbances* (1969), based on his work in the psychiatric hospital of the Karl Marx University in Leipzig. Kohler has edited a book, *Music Therapy: Theory and Methods* (1971) which deals with practical questions in music therapy. Both books basically are oriented toward a social-psychological theory of mental illness (DeBeir, 1974).

In Austria, since 1959 the Austrian Association for Promoting Music Therapy has been in existence, with its founder, Edith Koffer-Ullrich, as leader. Koffer-Ullrich had studied in the USA prior to this time, and returned to Vienna to begin her own training course for music therapists at the Vienna Academy for Music and Art. It was the first formal training course for music therapy in Europe, and is now directed (1975) by A. Schmolz. It is a three-year course, stressing mostly clinical applications, and following an orientation which is basically Freudian, or psychoanalytic. The association as yet does not publish a journal, but articles are published in other professional journals (DeBeir).

In France an Institute for Music Therapy was founded in 1969 as a part of the National Center for Research and Applications for Psychomusical Techniques. The institute was directed by J. Jost, a physician who stresses treatment of psychotic patients through music listening.

Francoise and Alfred Braunner have established another institute, "Groupement de Recherches Practiques pour l"Enfance," which stresses the use of music and rhythm in the treatment of autistic children. One book, *Music, Psychology, and Psychotherapy*, published by Guilhot in 1964, dealt with the contributions of music to psychotherapy. Ten years later, the first conference on music therapy in France was held in Paris (1974).

In Switzerland a committee was founded in 1971 to coordinate music therapy activities and interests in that country. This occurred during the first Swiss Forum for Music Therapy, at Lenk. The Forum continues to hold annual meetings, under the leadership of K. Pahlen and consists of meetings and addresses by music therapists, both Swiss and from other countries. Three Swiss authors have published books on music therapy: Alice Kundig, *The Experience of Music in a Psychological and Psychotherapeutic Approach with Particular Considerations on its Compensatory Function* (1961); Therese Hirsch, *Music and Reeducation Experiences of Music Therapy for Profoundly Mentally Retarded Children*, (1966); and H. E. Durrer, *Music and Rhythm With Psychically Disturbed Infants* (1954).

In Yugoslavia, a branch of the group called the International Association for Social Psychiatry, has been founded to emphasize music therapy and to attempt to establish an international organization of music therapy. A psychiatrist, Breitenfeld, who works principally with alcoholic patients, has been instrumental in promoting this group, and has organized meetings in Zagreb for several years, during the 1970's. The first meeting of an "International Congress on Music Therapy" was held in 1970, and an international board of directors included music therapists from several countries, including England and America. However, the hoped-for publication of a journal had not materialized by the mid-1970's (DeBeir).

In Belgium, music therapy as an organized discipline was in its infancy in 1973. Mark DeBeir, who furnished much of the information in the preceding paragraphs, obtained American music therapy certification in 1974 (along with a masters degree in therapy from F.S.U.), and returned to begin work in music therapy at Leven. According to DeBeir, there is as yet no unified movement in the field of music therapy in Europe, but there is an observable increase of interest in the field in many places. Except for England and Austria, however, there are as yet no training programs of significance in Europe, and this is the greatest need. (We have noted above that some training programs have been explored in Holland and in Berlin, but not established with any great firmness as yet.) DeBeir states that while there are a wide variety of approaches being used in music therapy in European countries, the most prevalent theoretical foundation seems to be in the Freudian, or classical psychoanalytical model. As yet, very few if any therapists employ music on a behavioral model, i.e., using behavior modification techniques, but this is perhaps ". . . because behavior therapy itself is rather a recent phenomenon in Europe" (DeBeir, 1974).

As observed earlier, music therapy has been developing in Australia for many years, and in recent years, in Japan. What about Red China, Russia, and India? The author has seen an article in Esperanto in a magazine devoted to the Esperanto movement (development of an international language), concerning music therapy in mainland China, and has observed a few articles appearing in journals concerning psychology of music research in Russia. It has also been observed that many of the mystical ideas of Indian psychics have found their way into modern psychotherapy and even into modern music therapy. Transcendental meditation, or TM, for one, is one basis for relaxation and meditation techniques used by psychotherapists, and perhaps is similar to the bases for music therapists advocating the use of music to achieve "altered states of consciousness" during deep meditation and relaxation to music. (Bonny and Savary, 1973).

The idea of music therapy certainly does seem to be "an idea whose time has arrived" all around the world which should continue to develop and to make a contribution toward solving not only the everyday problems of mankind, but also, perhaps toward solving some of the larger problems encountered, and even manufactured on earth by man.

SUMMARY

Music therapists today are professional health workers who adopt the same general code of ethics of all health workers. This code centers around dedication to the relief of suffering in fellow human beings and the protection of the individual human rights of such persons. Professional music therapists also are dedicated to the use of music as their basic tool in working with those who are their clients.

Music is a term which encompasses many things, including an extremely wide variety of activities and stimuli. Music is the thing which makes music therapists MUSIC therapists, and these therapists also are unique in their possession of such a special tool as music. If nothing else, music therapists make use of music as a form of communication which may enhance the development of a warm, helping relationship with clients. But music, skillfully applied as structure, as a reinforcing activity of great power, and as a time-ordered stimulator and facilitator of human activity, does differentiate music therapists from other types of therapists and special teachers.

Music therapists may be thought of as "generalists" with a "special medium," in some ways comparable to other such generalists in the activity therapy field, and in contrast to some therapists who are specialists in terms of client populations they work with, but generalists with respect to the media they employ, such as education.

With respect to the development of music therapy around the world it was noted that interest in the field has grown within the last two decades (1960's, and 1970's), and that music therapy in some form is now found on almost every major continent of the earth. Major developments have occurred in the United States, and in Europe, England has led the way. Developments were specifically noted in South America, in Australia, and in Japan, as well as in several European countries. Only brief references have been noted from Russia, China, and India, but it has become apparent to some that music therapy seems to be an idea whose time has come. Its continued growth and development toward constructive solutions of problems of mankind on this earth is expected.

CHAPTER 5

MUSIC THERAPY EDUCATION AND TRAINING

DEVELOPMENT OF PROFESSIONAL STANDARDS FOR MUSIC THERAPY

WHEN the NAMT was organized (1950) several diverse but interested groups of people converged at a national music teachers organization meeting (MTNA, Washington, D.C.). Music teachers in private instruction, at college or university and conservatory level, and from the public school sector, along with a few early pioneer music therapists in the field met to discuss the possibility of organizing a national association. Government officials, especially those concerned with the hospitals for war veterans, were also present and one of them (Ray Green) was elected the first president of the new NAMT. There was a growing demand for music specialists in hospitals, especially the veterans' hospitals, and in certain clinical settings for handicapped children as well. This demand was beginning to make itself felt not only among professional musicians and music teachers, but also at the university level, where students began to ask for specialized training in this new field of music therapy. Thus the NAMT answered a need and brought together a number of people from quite varied and divergent fields. A few physicians, psychiatrists, psychologists, and occupational therapists also were among the first founding fathers of NAMT.

Fortunately, from these several sources a strong leadership developed with NAMT from the beginning. In 1953, discussions about setting standards in training music therapists culminated in the setting up of the Minimum Educational Requirements. These were based on a four-year baccalaureate degree program with an additional six months of clinical internship to be taken in approved psychiatric hospitals. By 1953, at least three universities already were offering specialized training for music therapists (Michigan State University, Kansas University, and The University of the Pacific), and the agreement to set standards at the baccalaureate level already was a major concession for one of the schools (Kansas) which had begun its training at the masters' degree level.

The clinical training requirement in a psychiatric hospital was not only in recognition of the first and largest area of demand for music therapists (veterans' hospitals, especially) but also based on the belief that such hospitals provided the broadest possible kind of clinical experience. Some psychiatric hospitals other than veterans' not only treated adult men and women patients but also children, and had in some instances not only psychiatric patients, but also mentally retarded patients. (Today, NAMT has approved other types of clinical training centers — mostly of the mentally retarded type.)

It should be noted that many hours of conference and correspondence among NAMT members, educators and clinicians alike, were needed to get to these fundamental levels of agreement on academic and clinical education for music therapists. And, it was several years before conformity with generally agreed-upon procedures was finally accomplished, even though the number of universities offering training was still under ten. For one thing, some university programs interpreted the six-month clinical experience requirement as being divisible into two or three periods, interspersed with the last two years of academic training. The clinical training centers and therapists, however, discouraged this type of splitting-up of the internship, based upon the fact that internships for a clinical center were a mixed blessing, and were considered to be done on the basis of mutual benefit. Interns were said to only become useful as fledgling therapists after about three months in the training, and if this WERE to be separated into two or more segments, the value of the intern would be lost just at the time he was becoming useful! Some educators also objected to the division of clinical training on the grounds that the interns could not take full advantage of the academic (on-campus) training if they began it before the senior (or last) year's professionul courses were given. In any case, the agreement was finally reached, and has been sustained up to the present, that the six-months' clinical training should follow the academic training, and should be a continuous, residential type of placement.

In the first years of clinical training, students were fortunate if they were provided room and board; today, however, most internship centers provide living allowances (stipends) for interns.

Another landmark in the professional development of Music Therapy through NAMT action occurred in 1957, when registration-certification requirements were begun. NAMT minimum education requirements were the basis for the granting of the Registered Music Therapist classification, but, as was common in many other professional organizations, a period of three years was allowed before education requirements became the *only* qualifications for registration. This was known as the "grandfathers" clause, which allowed all persons who were full-time employees in Music Therapy and had been so for at least three years up to 1960, to become registered on that basis. From 1960, then, only those persons completing the basic four-year course and internship — OR ITS EQUIVALENT — have been registered in NAMT and certified as qualified therapists. Enforcement of these requirements has been by committee within NAMT, and by a national accrediting organization for departments and schools of music in universities (National Association of Schools of Music).

(In 1960, as part of the writer's Presidential address at the NAMT Conference in San Francisco, the steps taken by NAMT in its first ten years towards developing professional standards were described as a process analagous to the treatment of a patient, with the profession of M.T. being the "patient" and NAMT being the "therapist." It was concluded that the patient was getting well, and beginning to reach some maturity. However, since maturing is a continual, life-time process, the music therapy profession in the USA should be viewed as still developing, and trying to mature (Michel, 1961).

Education requirements agreed upon for the four-year (plus internship) program included a "core" of professional music therapy courses. These were to be based upon other, foundational courses, principally in the behavior science field, as well as in music skills and knowledge fields. These professional courses were to be taught only by qualified persons, that is, someone who had adequate training and experience in music therapy. Later, this was interpreted as meaning a person who qualified as an RMT and who had had post-graduate training in the field.

An overall look at the four-year degree course sanctioned by NAMT reveals that only minimum requirements are stated. This is intentional, since every university has its own special requirements to be met. A look at the programs now offered in the approved universities in the USA will reveal quite some variety in special subject courses offered, particularly in the core course area. But the four-year minimum program also is apparent. Looking at it generally, one might divide the subject matter into two or three large categories: music courses (a little less than one-half of the requirements); therapy courses; and therapy-related courses (a little more than one-half of the total course-hours required). The NAMT groups the subject matter into seven categories, as follows: 1) General education — thirty semesters hours (also one-fourth of the total — which includes language, history, science, and other subjects considered essential for the general education of all university students); 2) Functional dance activities — four semester hours (this is an attempt to assure basic instruction in the important area of bodily movement responses to music); 3) Music — sixty semester hours (subdivided into music theory, music history, piano, voice, guitar, orchestral and band instruments, conducting, arranging, and recreational music); 4) Sociology and anthropology — eight semester hours (considered foundational from the behavior sciences); 5) Psychology — ten semester hours (with general and abnormal psychology required, the remainder selected from a fairly wide range of psychology courses); 6) Music therapy — ten semester hours (this includes psychology of music, influence of music on behavior, music in therapy, and hospital orientation courses); and 7) General electives — six semester hours (allowing for some choice of subjects by individual students). (TOTAL: 128 semester hours.) The hospital orientation course is not considered to be the same as the required internship, but a preparatory course for clinical affiliation. However, many universities do give academic credit for the clinical training. Over the past ten years, these internships have become increasingly structured through cooperative efforts between clinical centers and universities, with resultant justification for giving academic credit.

A closer look at the area of music subjects shows that there are similarities to the American requirements for music teachers who plan to work in the school systems, either at primary or secondary level. However, it is not so evident that the requirements in piano, voice, and organ are translated in many schools to mean a required level of performance proficiency by each student on the instrument of his choice, not *only* in piano and voice. The piano and voice proficiencies, for those students not having specialized in these performance areas, are interpreted as basic or elemental proficiencies. The organ requirement has now been dropped from NAMT standards, since it is seldom the practice today to require the music therapist to also be the chapel organist in hospitals. However, some universities do still offer a basic methods type of course in organ to familiarize students with the many varieties of modern keyboard-electronic instruments.

Orchestral and band instruments now may include study on guitar, or other informal-social type instruments. Recreational music implies further development of informal music skills such as leading group singing, playing percussion instruments, and teaching music listening enjoyment. Conducting and arranging (orchestration) courses also are geared, where possible, to the demands of the great variety of patients, often musically illiterate, found by music therapists in their clinical experience.

As for the core professional courses, the content is not prescribed by NAMT, but NAMT has done much to insure *some* uniformity through its annual conferences on both national and regional levels. These conferences also assure that some stimulation and competition between various universities may develop in what is taught in the professional courses. The publication of annual yearbooks from 1951-1961, a professional journal since 1962, and finally, most recently the book, *Music in Therapy* (1968), edited by E. Thayer Gaston, and compiled by ten educators in music therapy from around the USA, all have provided some central focus to the content of professional music therapy courses.

What is taught in the other professional core courses does vary from university to university to some degree. For example, some schools interpret the Hospital Orientation to mean a three-month summer placement of students in a clinical setting as a sort of pre-clinical training experience (between the last two years). The psychology of music courses also vary somewhat, with different universities using different basic textbooks. However, it may be said that generally a research and scientific approach is followed in terms of considering the basic interactions of music and man. For example, course content often includes a study of the physiology of the ear and hearing, as well as the usual considerations of communication aspects of music (mood, etc.), music learning, music aptitude and ability, and tests developed for music responses in these areas. A second course may specifically develop a research approach to psychology of music problems, and may provide a chance to try out approaches in "mini-research" problems.

Curriculum requirements and standards under the NAMT have been regularly reviewed and changes considered and made over the entire history of NAMT, but perhaps these are matters which are seldom if ever actually up-to-date, or planned for the future well enough. Controversies over the years have revolved around such questions as: what kind of basic music skills SHOULD every music therapist possess? Should all be proficient at the keyboard? Mostly by tacit agreement, this has been translated that only fundamental proficiency at the keyboard is necessary; however, it has sometimes been translated into implying a similar proficiency on the principal instrument of the individual student.

A master's degree thesis (Galloway, 1966) explored differences of opinion among various categories of members of the NAMT: therapists, directors of clinical programs, interns, and college professors. Galloway discovered a number of areas of disagreement, especially as to which musical skills should be brought by the intern to his clinical training. There also was a division of opinion as to exactly what should be taught during the clinical training period, particularly with regard to music skills. Galloway found a difference of opinion regarding the teaching of basic research and evaluation techniques for young music therapists, i.e., more being demanded by the interns than thought necessary by some clinicians. Results of this study have influenced the courses and course content at several universities.

The matter of what the content of professional courses should be is a most important one. It also is where current practice in the field probably ought to carry considerable influence. However, education should be something more than a mirror-image of current practice. Universities traditionally have been expected to furnish leadership in terms of research and innovation, which in turn may affect current practices. Notwithstanding the quest of university students for "relevance" and of the research programs being carried out in clinical centers, fresh ideas should originate from the sometimes isolated, but independent "Ivory Towers" of the university.

Research, both at the university and the clinical level, and sometimes cooperatively carried out by both, is an important matter which determines what the education of music therapists is and will be in the future. Therefore, perhaps the most important aspect aimed at in music therapy education is the development of a scientific, or research attitude. Not only must students be able to continue to learn and grow in their field once formal education has been completed, but they also must know how to objectively evaluate their daily work with patients. There is an attempt to teach this attitude and its practical realization in not only the foundational courses, but also in the professional core courses (Michel, Madsen, 1969). Perhaps this is the hallmark today of music therapy in the USA, and one reason why it is gaining the increasing attention and approval of the medical and psychological professions. It very well may be why music therapy today is a field whose time has arrived!

SUMMARY

Education and training of music therapists, like the education and training of other professionals, depends upon a definition of the profession, as well as an awareness of what the professional person does in his daily work. It is a combination not only of the here and now but also of the then (past) and the future. Education and training should not only reflect the past and the present practices, it should point the way for future development.

Music therapy has been defined as a behavioral science. This means that the foundation of training and education in music therapy must be not only in music but equally strong in the behavior sciences themselves. Professional courses in music therapy must bring music and behavior science together in the teaching of techniques and skills in music therapy. They also should teach the scientific attitude, for research as well as for clinical practice. These courses must also teach the theories behind practicies in music therapy to give the student the proper perspective and depth he will need as a professional person.

A brief outline of the development of professional standards for music therapy through the NAMT in America has been presented. It is hoped that the struggles and mistakes of the NAMT, as well as its positive accomplishments can be of some help to others who are concerned with the same kind of development in other parts of the world.

WHAT ABOUT THE FUTURE?

The field of music therapy continues to experience changes which parallel and are derived from the changes in the whole field of health, especially mental health. They reflect the rapidly increasing demands for health services in our society. This is not only a function of the population explosion but also of the increasing public recognition of and responsibility for health services to which individuals in our society are entitled.

What are some of these changes? They center around the fact that the role of the registered music therapist, similar to other health workers, can no longer be solely that of a *therapist*. Why? Because we probably cannot produce enough professionally qualified *therapists*, through our present means, to meet the projected demands. Today's and tommorow's registered music therapist must not be only a therapist but also a person who can teach part of his techniques to others, so that his influence may extend to begin to meet greater demands. This does not mean he will "give away" his craft. It does mean he will have to learn how to demonstrate, to teach, to consult, and to supervise music therapy functions with others who have not been specifically or professionally trained in music therapy. This may be comparable to the changing role of the registered nurse, resulting in the development of the licensed practical nurse and other types of nurses' aides.

A few years ago, Braswell advocated that music therapists be given more intense training as *group* therapy specialists (1961). Madsen proposed revision of the basic professional curriculum for music therapy at the bachelor's degree level: mainly, that there should be a de-emphasis on the music theory and music performance subject areas which have kept music therapy students in the same track as students studying to be performers or teachers, and an increased emphasis on behavioral science subjects (1965). Neither of these proposals were entirely adequate for the trends which have developed today, although both have merit, and are being activated in some university programs.

Probably more training in group therapy and more emphasis upon behavioral science with less in applied music *should* be implemented in undergraduate music therapy education, but there also should be provision for training the music therapy student in such probable future roles as Supervisor, Consultant, and Teacher of other professionals and sub-professionals in the helping services. The RMT should learn how to extend his effectiveness by sharing and teaching his skills with such persons. Who are some of these persons?

Reports by students in an introductory course taught by the author at the University of New Mexico (1966-1967) demonstrated how they could learn certain music therapy techniques and apply them, at least in a elementary way, and with the presumption of "back-up" assistance (consultation) from a professional music therapist, the projects ranged from "The Influence of Music on Disruptive Behavior" in a junior high school band rehearsal to "The Role of Music in Therapy for Patients with Chronic Obstructive Lung Disease." Several were concerned with applications for retarded children, and others dealt with applications for behaviorally disturbed children, both in schools and in guidance centers. There were studies which involved applications of music therapy techniques for children with speech disorders, and others involving applications for elderly patients in a nursing home. There was even an attempt to relate music therapy techniques to problem singers in a fourth-grade music class. One report was a case study of music therapy for a young suicidal, depressed patient in a county hospital psychiatric ward.

The "students" who made the reports included public school music teachers, private music teachers, classroom teachers — both in general and special education, a reading specialist teacher, a guidance counselor, and speech and hearing therapists. From their experiences it was concluded that they seemed to gain respect for music therapy, but also recognized the need for professional guidance by registered music therapists if further applications were to be made.

The sharing of special knowledge, so important and essential in the expanding health programs and needs of today and tomorrow, is one step in the direction of cooperation. It is to be hoped that music therapists will increase their effectiveness by learning how to share their special knowledge and skills with others. It is also important to learn the special skills and knowledge of other therapy and education specialists which may extend the effectiveness of music therapy. There is a need to recognize this changing role of the RMT from that of the competent practicing clinician and team member to that of competent clinician-educator-consultant. This also implies a need for change in the educational preparation of music therapists. It could be one of the greatest challenges facing the field of music therapy today.

Another way now being considered for meeting the needs of the profession for more trained personnel is the development of music therapy "aides," "associates," or "assistants." Such persons might be trained in community colleges or technical schools. Several hospitals in Georgia are now using as music therapy assistants persons who have basic music skills and who sometimes hold a music degree in another area of specialization and who work on the job with a registered music therapist. At one of the hospitals, Southwestern Georgia State, music therapists have given training to nurses aides who work on the wards directly with the patients. So far, the utilization of such personnel to amplify and reinforce the music therapy programs seems to be working well.

Expanding horizons in music therapy reach toward other new roles for music therapists in the community. As Harvey Hall puts it, "Music therapy (is) moving out (of institutional practice) into the mainstream" (1969). Not only are music therapists finding themselves working in programs with disadvantaged children and with other persons in "inner city" situations, they are working as special education "resource" persons or consultants in the public schools, and they are finding themselves in demand in other community-based programs like comprehensive community mental health, private and semi-private convalescent or nursing homes, and rehabilitation centers for the physically handicapped. More and more music therapists are finding themselves in demand for work with juvenile delinquents and with other children and youth with special behavioral and/or learning problems.

Much of the current work and future work of music therapists is being determined by an increasing amount of research being done in the field, as well as in the laboratory. It is possible that future music therapists may even choose research as their specialty in the field. Certainly the development of the field will depend upon the continuation and expansion of valid research.

Earlier in this chapter it was noted that research training is an important part of music therapy courses, even at the undergraduate level. Graduate research already has begun to influence the development of the field, but much more research which takes place in the field as well as in the university setting is needed if music therapy procedures are to be validated and extended.

SUMMARY

The future of music therapy definitely lies in the mainstream of the health related services rather than in traditional institutions. The mainstream of health care itself now is certainly to be seen more often in the community. Mental health clinics, half-way houses for those being reintegrated into the community from institutional life, physical therapy rehabilitation centers, special learning centers for those with special handicaps such as visual, hearing, or emotional-social problems, and activity-learning centers for adult special education are some of the community centers where music therapists are working and will be working in the future. Special education programs within the schools or as a part of school systems also will be employing more music therapists. It is possible that these new opportunities for music therapists will indicate a need for specialization in the training of music therapists, as well as the need for the roles of consultant and teacher already mentioned.

Research will be necessary to define the roles of music therapists as well as to direct the most fruitful ways in which music therapy may be applied. For this reason, as well as the necessity for the learning of a research approach by *any* clinical person, will make research training an increasingly vital part of the music therapist's education.

The future of music therapy has already begun. The direction and expansion of the field will be determined by the responsible, accountable music therapists going into practice, who will need to be like other good health care professionals: both scientific and compassionate in their approaches to helping other persons. The future music therapist is fortunate to have at hand his music and musical skills as his therapeutic tools. Man has long enjoyed the scientific, esthetic, and emotional aspects of music. In this twentieth century it is the music therapist who is able to put these components of music to work in helping those in society who need help.

REFERENCES

A Career in Music Therapy (Pamphlet): Lawrence, Kansas: National Association for Music Therapy, Inc., 1975.

Alexander, Shana: Getting Old in Kids' Country. *Newsweek*, November 11, 1974, 124.

Alvin, Juliette: *Music Therapy*. London: John Baker, 1966.

Alvin, Juliette: *Music for the Handicapped Child*. London, New York: Oxford University Press, 1968.

Alvin, Juliette: *Report on the Research Project on Music Therapy With Severely Subnormal Boys*. London: The British Society for Music Therapy, 1969.

A Survey of Potential Needs and Uses of Music Therapy at a Juvenile Detention Center: Unpublished Class Study. Tallahassee, Fla.: The Forida State University Music Therapy Information Retrieval Center, 1965.

Bonny, Helen: The Use of Music in Psychedelic (LSD) Psychotherapy. *Journal of Music Therapy*, 9, 2, 64, 1971.

Bonny, Helen and Savary, Louis: *Music and Your Mind*. New York: Harper & Row, 1973.

Bosco, Bonnie K.: The Use of Radio Remote Control for the Contingent Application of Music in a Therapy Setting with an Autistic Child. Unpublished Masters Thesis. Tallahassee, Fla.: The Florida State University, 1974.

Boucher, Stanley: Developments in Community Mental Health. Unpublished Lecture to University of New Mexico Medical School. Alburquerque, New Mexico, 1967. (On file: The Florida State University Music Therapy Information Retrieval Center.)

Braswell, Charles: Psychiatric Music Therapy: A Review of the Profession. *Music Therapy 1961*. Lawrence, Kansas: Allen Press, 1962.

British Journal of Music Therapy: Published three times a year by the British Society for Music Therapy, 48 Lancaster Road, London, Nc 4At, England.

Clausell, Aaronetta E.: Music Therapy to Train Blind Children in Auditory Discrimination of Street Sounds. Unpublished Masters Thesis. Tallahassee, Fla.: The Florida State University, 1974.

Davis, Geraldine, Slonin, S., and Walker, J.: Music Therapy Case Studies in Speech Therapy. Unpublished. Tallahassee, Fla.: The Florida State University Music Therapy Information Retrieval Center, 1967.

DeBeir, Mark G.: Music Therapy in Europe. Unpublished. Tallahassee, Fla.: The Florida State University Music Therapy Information Retrieval

Center, 1974.

Dobbs, Jack C. B.: *The Slow Learner and Music: A Handbook for Teachers.* London: Oxford University Press, 1970.

Durrer, Hans D.: *Musik und Rhythmik bei Psychisch Gehemmten Kindern des Vorschulalters.* Luzern: Institut fur Heilpedagogik, 1954.

Eagle, Charles T.: Music and LSD: An Empirical Study. *Journal of Music Therapy,* 9, 1, 1972.

Galloway, Herbert F.: Articulation Problems in the Academic and Clinical Training of Music Therapists. Unpublished. Masters Thesis. Tallahassee, Fla.: The Florida State University, 1966.

Gaston, E. Thayer (Ed.): *Music in Therapy.* New York: Macmillan, 1968.

Gerits, Leoburt: Training in Sound Perception of Severely Deaf Children, Combined with Dance, Rhythmic and Expressive Movements. Unpublished. St. Michielsgestel, Netherlands: Institute voor Doven, 1967.

Glasser, William: *Reality Therapy: A New Approach to Psychiatry.* New York: Harper and Row, 1965.

Greenfield, Dianne: Music Therapy at an Easter Seal Rehabilitation Center: A Demonstration Project. Unpublished. Tallahassee, Fla.: The Florida State University Music Therapy Information Retrieval Center, 1971.

Gregory, Dianne: Improvement of Auditory Memory in Severely Emotionally Disturbed Children. Unpublished. Tallahassee, Fla.: The Florida State University Music Therapy Information Retrieval Center, 1970.

Guide to the Order Sheet: Pamphlet MF-188, Rev. 4., Topeka, Kansas: The Menninger Foundation, 1950.

Guilhot, Jean: *Musique, Psychologie, et Psychotherapie.* Paris: Editions Sociales Francaises, 1964.

Hall, Harvey: Music Therapy Moves into the Community. *Newletter.* Great Lakes Regional Chapter of the National Association for Music Therapy, 1969 (Winter). Central Office, NAMT, P.O. Box 610, Lawrence, Kansas 66044.

Hanser, Suzanne: The Effects of Contingent Music Upon the Behavior of a Group of Junior High School Students. Unpublished Masters Thesis. Tallahassee, Fla.: The Florida State University, 1972.

Hirsch, Therese: *Musique et Reeducation: Experiences de Therapie Musicale avec des Enfants Profondement Debiles.* Neuchatel: Delachaux, 1966.

Holthaus, Clemens: *Muziektherapie.* Amsterdam-Brussels: Agon Elsevier, 1970.

Irwin, Constance E.: Songs and Music Coding to Improve Sound Blends in Cleft Palate Speech. Unpublished. Tallahassee, Fla.: The Florida State University Music Therapy Information Retrieval Center, 1971.

Irwin, Constance E., Plumb, Ina J., and Walker, J.: The Use of Music as an Aid in Teaching R and S Sounds to Mentally Retarded Children. Unpublished. Tallahassee, Fla.: The Florida State University Music Therapy Information Retrieval Center, 1971.

Irwin, Constance E.: The Use of Music in a Language Development Program for

Mentally Retarded Children, with Emphasis on Down's Syndrome. Unpublished Masters Thesis. Tallahassee, Fla.: The Florida State University, 1971.

Josef, Kurt: *Musik als Hilfe in der Erziehung Geistig Behinderter.* Berlin: Marhold, 1970.

Journal of Music Therapy, Published quarterly since 1963 by the National Association for Music Therapy, P.O. Box 610, Lawrence, Kansas, 66044.

Kohler, Christa (Ed.): *Musiktherapie: Theorie und Methodik.* Jena: Fischer, 1971.

Kundig, Alice: *Das Musikerlebnis in Psychologischer und Psychotherapeutischer Sischt mit Besonderer Berucksichtigung seiner Kompensatorischen Funktion.* Winterthur: Keller, 1962.

Lievegoed, B.C.J.: *Jaat-Rhythme-Melodie: Gröndslagen voor een Therapeutisch Gebruik van Muzikale Elementen.* Zeist: Vrij Geestesley, 1939.

Lim, Beatrice C.: The Effect of Music on the Self-esteem of Hospitalized Psychiatric Patients. Unpublished Masters Thesis. Tallahassee, Fla.: The Florida State University, 1974.

Madsen, Clifford K.: A New Music Therapy Curriculum. *Journal of Music Therapy,* 2, 3, 1965, 83-85.

Madsen, Clifford K. and Madsen, Charles H.: Music as a Behavior Modification Technique with a Juvenile Delinquent. *Journal of Music Therapy,* 5, 3, 1968, 69-71.

Madsen, Clifford K., Michel, Donald E., and Madsen, Charles H.: The Use of Music Stimuli in Teaching Language Discrimination with Head Start Students. In *Research in Music Behavior,* C.K. Madsen, D. Greer, and C.H. Madsen, Jr., (Eds.). New York: Teachers College Press, Columbia University, 1975.

Masserman, Jules: *Modern Therapy of Personality Disorders.* Dubuque, Iowa, Wm. C. Brown, 1966.

Michel, Donald E.: A Study of the Sedative Effects of Music for Acutely Disturbed Patients in a Mental Hospital. Unpublished Masters Thesis. Lawrence, Kansas: University of Kansas, 1950. (Summary published in *Music Therapy 1951,* Lawrence, Kansas: Allen Press, 1952, 182-183.)

Michel, Donald E.: A Survey of 375 Cases in Music Therapy at a Mental Hospital. *Music Therapy 1958,* Lawrence, Kansas: Allen Press, 1959, 166-176. (See also: Concluding Report: A Survey of 375 Cases in Music Therapy. In *Music Therapy 1959,* 137-152.)

Michel, Donald E.: . . . And the Patient Gets Well (Presidential Address). *Music Therapy 1960.* Lawrence, Kansas: Allen Press, 1961, 3-8.

Michel, Donald E.: Music Therapy in the Southeastern United States. *Music Therapy 1962.* Lawrence, Kansas: Allen Press, 1963, 204.

Michel, Donald E.: Professional Profile: The NAMT Member and His Clinical Practices in Music Therapy. *Journal of Music Therapy,* 2, 4, 1965, (December), 124-129.

Michel, Donald E.: Music Therapy in Speech Habilitation of Cleft Palate Children. In *Music in Therapy*, E.T. Gaston (Ed.). New York: The Macmillan Co., 1968.

Michel, Donald E. and Madsen, Clifford K.: Examples of Research in Music Therapy as a Function of Undergraduate Education. *Journal of Music Therapy*, 6, 1, 1969, 22-25.

Michel, Donuld E. and Gray, Richard M.: A Pioneering Music Therapy Program Effort After Twenty Four Years. Unpublished Paper. Tallahassee, Fla.: The Florida State University Music Therapy Information Retrieval Center, 1969.

Michel, Donald E. and Martin, Dorothea: Music and Self-esteem: Research with Disadvantaged Problem Boys in an Elementary School. *Journal of Music Therapy*, 7, 4, 1970, 124-127.

Michel, Donald E.: Self-esteem and Academic Achievement in Black Junior High School Students: Effects of Automated Guitar Instruction. *Council for Research in Music Education Bulletin*, 24, 1971, 15-23.

Michel, Donald E.: Music Therapy: An Idea Whose Time Has Arrived Around the World. *Journal of Music Therapy*, 8, 3, 1971.

Michel, Donald E. and Farrell, Dorothea M.: Music and Self-esteem: Disadvantaged Problem Boys in an All Black Elementary School. *Journal of Research in Music Education*, 21, 1970, pp. 80-85.

Michel, Donald E. and May, Nancy H.: The Development of Music Therapy Procedures with Speech and Language Disorders. *Journal of Music Therapy*, 11, 2, 1974, 74-80.

Music Therapy as a Career: Pamphlet published by the National Association for Music Therapy, Lawrence, Kansas: 1975.

Nordorff, Paul and Robbins, Clive: *Music Therapy for Handicapped Children*. New York: Steiner Publications, 1965.

Pontvik, Adolph: *Grundgedanken zur Psychischen Heilwirkung der Musik*. Zurich: Rascher, 1948.

Ross, Lynn: Music Therapy for A Stroke Victim. Unpublished. Tallahassee, Fla.: The Florida State University Music Therapy Information Retrieval Center, 1973.

Schmolz, Arnold: Lehrgang fur Musiktherapie an der Hochschule fur Musik und Darstellende Kunst. *Musik und Bildung*, 4, 1972, 408-410.

Schwabe, Christoph: *Musiktherapie bei Neurosen und Funktionellen Storungen*. Stuttgart: Fischer, 1972.

Seyle, Hans: *The Stress of Life*. New York: McGraw-Hill, 1956.

Seybold, Charles: The Value and Use of Music Activities in the Treatment of Speech Delay in Children. *Journal of Music Therapy*, 8, 3, 1971.

Snider, Arthur J.: Ten Myths About Aging. Sunday Scene, *San Francisco Chronical-Examiner*, Dec. 1, 1974, 45.

Stadsklev, Joan: The Use of Music with a Class of Cerebral Palsied Children. Unpublished. Tallahassee, Fla.: The Florida State University Music Therapy Information Retrieval Center, 1966.

Steele, Anita L.: The Community Music School: Flexibility and Accessibility. *Journal of Music Therapy*, 9, 3, 1972, 111.

Stephens, Ellen H.: The Effect of Music and Relaxation on the Anxiety Level of Alcoholics: A Pilot Study. Unpublished Masters Thesis. Tallahassee, Fla.: The Florida State University, 1974.

Tarnopol, Louis: *Learning Disorders in Children*. Boston: Little, Brown, 1971.

Teirich, Heinrich R. (Ed.): *Musik in der Medizin: Beitrage zur Musiktherapie*. Stuttgart: Fischer, 1958.

Unkefer, Robert F.: *Music Therapy in the Rehabilitation of the Adult Blind*. A Research Project Report. Topeka, Kansas: State Department of Social Welfare of Kansas, Services for the Blind, 1957.

Valett, Robert E.: *Programming Learning Disorders*. Palo Alto, California: Fearon Pub., 1969.

Van Stone, Joan K.: Personal Communication, 1975.

Van Stone, William W.: Peer Groups and Drug Rehabilitation. *Journal of Music Therapy*, 10, 1, 1973.

Walker, John B.: The Use of Music as an Aid in Developing Functional Speech in the Institutionalized Retarded. *Journal of Music Therapy*, 9, 1, 1972.

Webster's Seventh New Collegiate Dictionary: Springfield, Mass.: G.C. Merriam and Co., 1963.

Wilson, Brian: The Effect of Music and Verbal Mediation on the Learning of Paired-Associates by Institutionalized Retardates. Unpublished Masters Thesis. Tallahassee, Fla.: The Florida State University, 1971.

Wilson, Ellaine and Hendrick, Gail: Music Therapy and Speech Therapy: Development of Cooperative Interdisciplinary Techniques. Unpublished. Tallahassee, Fla.: The Florida State University Music Therapy Information Retrieval Center, 1971.

Wolfgart, Hans: *Das Orff-Schulwerk im Deinste der Erziehung und Therapie Behinderter Kinder*. Berlin: Marhold, 1971.

AUTHOR INDEX

SUBJECT INDEX

A

Accounting for changes through data observations in behavior disorders, 78
Activity therapists, 10, 16
Activity therapy, 8, 9-10
Adjunctive therapy, 8, 9
Adulthood, 65-66
 divisions of, 65
 when one approaches, 65
Advantages of music therapy, vii-ix
Alcoholics Anonymous, 80
Ancillary therapy, 9
Antabuse, 80
Anxiety of physically handicapped, 84
Appropriate language, use of, 29-30
Associations for Retarded "Citizens," 81
Attention to stimuli, 29
Attitude therapy, 9
Attitudes toward professional music therapist, 93
Auditory memory "sequencing," 21
Austrian Association for Promoting Music Therapy, 102

B

Beginnings of music therapy, 5
Behavior conditioning theories, 10
Behavior disorders of children, 15-16
Behavior goals, 71-72
 aids concentration, 71
 community involvement, 72
 development of leisure time skills, 72
 development of new interests, 72
 learn how it feels to relax, 71
 participation in activities, 72
 relaxation, 71
 socialization, 71
 verbal interaction, 71
Behavior goals in problems and treatment

of adults with behavior disorders, 71-72
"Behavior disorder" as synonym for "Mental illness," 15
Berlin Workshop on Music Therapy, 102
Bibliotherapy, 8
Birth trauma, 63
Borocourt Hospital, 100
Braille reading, 34, 35
"British Journal of Music Therapy," 100
British Society for Music Therapy, 99, 119

C

Canadian Association of Music Therapy, 99
Carnegie Foundation, 100
Children with repeated failure experiences, physical and environmental limitations, motivational problems, anxiety, erratic behavior, incomplete education and inadequate education, need special education, 63
Cleft palate children, 43
Cleveland Music School Settlement, 73
Community-based clinics and centers, 21-22
Community-based programs for adults, 72-75
Community School of Music and Arts at Mountain View, California, 73
Concepts of diagnostic labeling, 17-19
Concept of illness, 14-15
 disability, 14-15
 dislocation of equilibrium, 14-15
 disorder, 14-15
 distress, 14-15
 stress, 14-15
Concept of multiple handicaps, 16-17
Constructive use of leisure time of adults, 83
Continuation and expansion of valid

127